Embracing My Shadow

growing up lesbian in Nigeria

Unoma Azuah

Beaten Track
www.beatentrackpublishing.com

Embracing My Shadow

Published 2020 by Beaten Track Publishing
Copyright © 2020 Unoma Azuah

All rights reserved.

The moral right of the author has been asserted.

Paperback ISBN: 978 1 78645 373 0
eBook ISBN: 978 1 78645 374 7

Cover design: Nnanna David Ikpo

Beaten Track Publishing,
Burscough, Lancashire.
www.beatentrackpublishing.com

"When there is no enemy within, the enemies outside cannot hurt you."

—African Proverb

"I write for the still-fragmented parts in me, trying to bring them together. Whoever can read and use any of this, I write for them as well."

—Adrienne Rich,
Blood, Bread and Poetry:
The Location of the Poet

For Chinelo, my first love.

For my mother, Nwasoka Constance Nsugbe.

For my father, Peter Akaa Azuah.

Contents

Embracing My
Shadow

1. Snakes and Sins

I HAD SINNED. WE snuck out of our dormitory into the night, clung to each other as we thrust our tongues back and forth deep into each other's mouths. A tingling sensation made me grind my thighs together to ease the itch. I savored every taste of her tongue as I cradled her oval face in my palms. She steadied me with both of her hands behind my back, kneading her breasts against mine. Her cocoa butter fragrance hung between my lips and my nose. It was as good as the first time I had a taste of butter pecan ice cream.

That night, we saw what seemed like an endlessly long snake crawl by a few feet from where we stood. Nsukka snakes were said to be short; not this one. I shook, though I was not sure if it was because of a sudden wave of cold air or from the sight my eyes had fallen upon. My mind went back to the stories reverend sisters told us about Adam and Eve and how the snake made them fall into sin. I had fallen into sin again; maybe this was a sign from God to stop my sinful life. Shafts of moonlight shone along the snake's skin and made it seem more menacing. When it slithered off sight, I looked around for Star. She was gone.

Even for the time of the year, Nsukka had been unusually cold. The previous night had been a warm, bright night—too tempting to resist cuddling with Star. I found her very alluring and wanted to explore the attraction. It was not entirely physical; she had a knack for weird or stupid jokes, which I found refreshing. She joked about how Lady Koi-koi—the ghost that haunted our dormitory—ran into her one night and broke down in tears. A bunch of us laughed in disbelief. Everybody was terrified of Lady Koi-koi, so it should have been the other way around. Star ought to have passed out or cried in terror. Instead, it was the ghost who became terrified and cried.

Star and I could not keep our hands off each other. There was usually no privacy, so we would often hide behind thick shrubs or find a dim, empty classroom. The shrubbery was our regular spot. On one of those nights, we were caressing and canoodling when a student stumbled upon us and screamed. Startled, I screamed too.

"What is it? A snake?" I asked, terrified.

"Unoma Azuah, is that you? Are you taking a dump? Who is that with you? What are you two doing inside the bush at this time of the night?" She started approaching us, and Star scurried off. Between being recognized and caught—and the possibility of a looming snake—I was upset.

"What is your business, Echi? Come closer and find out!"

"I will tell your school mother. This is where you all come to do bad things. God forgive you."

"Go to hell!"

"Hell is already your destination!" she flung back and hurried off.

I knew she must have shown up there to take a dump like most girls did when our pit toilets oozed with stench and smoke. I wanted to get to the dormitory before her, so I fled, screaming, "Snake! Snake! Snake!" to cover up what Echi might reveal to anyone. I ran to the girl nearest the door and grabbed her. Before I could firm up my grip around her, the whole dormitory was on a stampede. Everyone ran toward the end of the hall away from me.

"Where is the snake?" Ora, a girl with bulging eyes, yelled, running toward me.

"It is outside!" I yelled back. In confusion, they ran into one another. Some ran out through the side door of our dormitory. Some ran toward the main entrance but then changed their minds and ran to the end of the dormitory again. Some stopped short as their eyes fell on my face.

"Why were you shouting as if the snake was already here with us?" Chibu, one of the meanest senior students, asked, glaring at me.

"It was outside," I said in a near-whisper with my eyes to the floor.

"What were you doing outside?" she insisted.

"Nothing. I was just outside."

"What were you doing outside at this time of the night to have stumbled upon a snake that was minding its business?" Ife, another senior with shiny cheekbones, joined in the interrogation.

"Nothing."

"Go and kneel at the corner of my bunk bed," she shouted.

I kneeled down. Star must have been wiser and not uttered a word when she ran into the other wing of our dorm—the quieter side. Contemplating as I kneeled, the thought of the snake crept back into my mind. I had more questions. *Was it that there were no apples in the Garden of Eden? Why would that one apple from a snake tempt Eve enough to eat it and then give it to Adam? Maybe they were hungry and it was convenient to eat that one apple. But why didn't God know they were hungry? Instead, he banished them from the garden. If the garden was a paradise, why didn't God provide enough apples? Will God banish me too? Has he cursed me?*

I shook the thought from my mind just as senior Ife's snore soared to a high pitch and crashed with a snort. I rolled my eyes at her. My knees were already hurting, and I had to get up to ease the soreness. Besides, I was not planning to kneel throughout the night while she snored away in blissful slumber. With one last glance as I watched her chest rise like a weak wave, I tiptoed to my bunk bed.

The next day, I expected her to scold me for not kneeling until she woke up, but she acted as if we'd never met. That was a relief. I was still bothered about what I'd been doing in the bush with Star. It was a sin.

I decided to go to confession. I hadn't fulfilled my sacrament of breaking bread because I was avoiding confession, which was often awkward. Half of the time the priest seemed to struggle with what I was saying. One time, I started off, "Forgive me, Father, for I have sinned," then reeled off my sins, half of them muttered under my breath. He'd cleared his throat and told me that any sin that was not heard by God was not going to be forgiven. I tried again.

"Forgive me, Father, for I have sinned. I kissed and played with a girl. We groped each other too."

"What do you mean? Why would you kiss a girl? And which parts of your bodies did you touch?"

"I don't remember, Father."

"That is a horrible sin. It was the sin that destroyed Sodom and Gonorrhea. Did you put your finger inside her private part? Did you put your tongue inside her mouth?"

"Yes."

"Yes to which one of the two? Did you put your hand anywhere in the girl's private part?" he asked eagerly.

I was confused. He was a new priest, and that was my first time going to him for a confession. The other priest merely told me the same thing: the sin that destroyed Sodom and Gomorrah. But this one wanted details. He wanted to know more.

"No," I said.

"Don't!" he said in a rather loud voice. "I forgive you your sins. Go and sin no more. Sweep the chapel next Sunday and say ten Hail Marys."

I left the confessional more rattled than when I'd arrived. I needed a place to be alone, to talk to God himself. My bunk bed was the only place I could think of. I had planned to get into bed and cover myself with a thick cloth to avoid people. But as soon as I stepped into our dormitory, my school mother grabbed me by the collar of my dress and dragged me to her bed corner. School mothers were senior students who were supposed to be guardians and care for their school daughters. As far as I knew, they were mostly tyrants. Without telling me what I was guilty of, she asked me to kneel. It all made sense to me when I saw Echi scowling at me from a distance.

That same night, Star and my school mother got into a verbal brawl over me. Her impression was that Star baited me to do bad things with her. Little did she know that I wanted Star as much as she wanted me, but my young, naïve look and my baby face made people see me as blameless. Eventually, Star kept her distance.

2. Gathering Clouds

ONE OF MY earliest memories of childhood was watching rain clouds gather. The sky held me spellbound. I was sucked in, transported to another world. Even with the single drop of rain that landed on my left cheek, I was still staring into the clouds. The rumble of thunder started as if daring me to keep watching. I was in a trance. But my mother screeching my name pulled me away from the looming sky.

"Unomaaaaa! Where are you?"

"Mama, I am outside!"

"What are you doing outside? The storm is here! Quickly, get all the clothes before they get soaked in rain while you daydream like a possessed child."

I leaped up from the cold concrete slab where I was sitting and ran to gather our dried clothes. I was still struggling with balancing the huge pile of clothes in my arms when the rains tore the skies open. My mother was quick. She must have been watching from the window because, before I tripped on one of the loose pieces of clothing, she yanked the bundle away from me and told me to run inside the house. She threw the clothes on her bed and asked me to fold them neatly. When I was done, I joined her in the living room, where she was patching up my torn school uniform. I lay on the ground beside her and listened to her sing one of her favorite hymns: "How sweet the name of Jesus sounds." I was bombarded by my mother's crooning of her

Anglican hymns. They would often lull me to sleep. Soothed, I dozed off.

That stormy day, I had a strange dream about a woman in the water. Everything was blurry. I couldn't tell how long I'd lain on the floor, but my mother tapping me on my feet told me to go to bed. I mumbled an okay but just lay there. She nudged me again and told me I would catch a cold if I didn't get up and go to the bed. I grunted a yes but didn't move an inch. Then she scampered toward me and landed a resounding slap on my buttocks. I scrambled up and rubbed my aching rear. I mumbled in protest, and she swung around to face me.

"Did I hear you say something?" she asked, her right hand positioned to land me another spank.

"No, Mama!" I screamed and ran out to the corridor where I'd sat earlier.

"I thought so," she shouted after me. "When you catch a cold, it is me who will be running around to find you medication or take you to the hospital. Stubborn child!"

I waited a while to hear her resume her hymn so I knew the coast was clear. Whenever she was aggravated or acted as if she was annoyed with me, I gave her some distance because I felt as if she read my body language to see if I was being disrespectful. When that was the case, she either glared at me or flung the nearest object she could find at me. So I learned how to take myself away from her to prevent her from reading anything from my body.

She was on the second verse of her hymn when I made my way to her room, tiptoeing. She asked me why I was walking like that. I told her I didn't want to break into her song with my noisy steps. She laughed and agreed I do have noisy steps, particularly when I flapped my oversized flippers around the house. I smiled at her. I went into her room and crawled into her bed.

It was a strange world I found myself in. I was surrounded by what looked like a large body of water: an island. Then there was what looked like an abandoned palm nut plantation. Immediately, I screamed and started running. I was not sure if something was after me; as much as I yelled, there seemed to be no one around to help me find my way out of the maze. Out of breath, I ran onto a larger footpath and paused. I recognized the place as Ote, the palm nut plantation at Umunede. The ground was soft from a recent rain, and I had no shoes on. My legs seemed to absorb the moisture.

I started screaming again and ran and didn't stop until I stumbled into a palm wine tapper. I couldn't answer any of his questions. He wanted to know where I came from, what I was doing in the forest. I couldn't say. I started running again and stumbled out onto a path with a couple of women bearing firewood. There, the sun shone brighter, and its channels of light were reassuring.

Again, my mother's voice woke me up. "Are you having a nightmare?"

Still drowsy from sleep, I muttered, "No," and went back to sleep.

My earliest recollections of the palm nut plantation at Umunede were with my mother. We walked through Ote on a deep, grooved path to her school. On our way, just before we got to Ote, there was a huge, open field where I would usually disentangle my hand from my mother's tight grip and run wild, chasing butterflies and grasshoppers. She would often look back to gauge our distance, but I never waited long enough to lose sight of her. When her shadow seemed to be disappearing, I would tear into a run, and she would linger for me to catch up.

Umunede was one of the many towns my parents lived in. Because my father was a Nigerian soldier, he was often moved around different cities and towns. We had lived in towns in the

Midwestern part of Nigeria, the former Bendel State, and places like Ekpoma, Auchi, Uromi, Yauri, and then Umunede. It was not too long after our move to Umunede when my father died. I was six, and my younger brother, Ugonna was one. My father named him Orseer. I have two older siblings, Ofunne and Dada. We don't share the same father, but my father cared for them as if they were his children.

Some of my memories of my father are vivid. I remember watching him chew kola nut. The crunch in the sound of breaking nuts in his mouth was something I found quite delicious. They were lobes of nuts, so he was reluctant to give me any. He would say that I could swallow them by mistake and choke. When I insisted, he would chew a small piece and then put it into my mouth with his mouth. The taste it left, though bitter, remained something I craved years after our ritual of kola-nut-sharing ended. He gave me the acquired taste one needed to chew a bitter kola nut. I also remember him hitting two fingers on my butt to discipline me whenever I threw a tantrum. He had rather long fingers, which was not surprising because he was a tall man.

I didn't know much about him, yet he related to me as an everyday father would relate. He would speak his Tiv language to me for basic things like "Come and eat—*Va ya ruam*." Many of those I barely remember, but his muscular face stays etched on my mind. For days, he was away from home. I would be with a group of friends—children like me who lived in the same vicinity—but then I was often lost in thought, thinking about my father and wondering when he would be home. Those were the days I attempted writing, scribbling what I called *Questions for God*. My questions for God didn't seem to have an end.

My mother became frantic some days and stepped out of our one-bedroom apartment to scan the long stretch of the half-dirt road that ran beside our building. I was sure she was looking out for him. Except for the occasional times I ran into them in what seemed to be a wrestle, I knew she loved him as much as I did, though the story of how they met was startling. It happened during the Nigerian civil war when Biafra tried to secede from Nigeria.

This is my mother's story in her words:

It was a few years after my teacher's training certification, and I was teaching at Iselle-ukwu Girls' Grammar School. But with the crisis that started in the North, my mother asked that I come home and be closer to her. This was in late 1967. It was a warm Sunday afternoon, and I was about to scoop the first spoonful of rice when I heard this piercing scream and then a loud thud. At first, I thought it might be sudden thunder, but there were no signs of rain. I couldn't find my mother or any of my siblings in the house. Everywhere seemed very quiet. I was tempted to scoop a second spoon of rice, still thinking about the explosive sound, when my oldest sister ran in and announced that the Nigerian troops had arrived. They had snuck into Asaba and set up camp at St. Patrick's College.

My mother returned and suggested we run to her brother's house. We didn't make it. We had run for about a mile when we saw a troop of soldiers in a pickup truck pointing their guns at us. They rounded us up and marched us to St. Patrick's. I was surprised on arrival. It seemed as if the whole Asaba town was there. St. Patrick's College had been made into a camp for civilians. My mother's panic showed on her face. She searched the crowd, hoping to see my second older sister and my younger brother. They had gone to visit an ill relative and had not been with us when we fled the house.

We spent months in the camp. Food was rationed, and we couldn't wash for days on end. One day, with no warning, the women and girls were separated from the men. The women were taken to St. Joseph's Mission near NECAB, while the men and boys were left at St. Patrick's College. We hadn't seen my brother yet.

We hadn't walked that far, less than five miles, when somebody snatched my hand away from my mother's and butted his gun on my shoulder. I shivered with fear and couldn't look that soldier in his eyes. He told me to step out of the crowd and follow him. My mother pleaded with him to take her instead. He ignored her and started dragging me out of the crowd. I didn't think twice. I took off. I ran as fast as I could. I knew somewhere at the back of my mind that even if he tried to shoot me, he was likely to miss. He didn't shoot. Instead, he raced toward me. I got lost in the crowd. I didn't know where I was running to, but I knew I had to escape from the soldier. After a comfortable distance of sprinting, I stopped running.

Out of breath, I was still cautious because the explosions continued. I stumbled upon a boy and a girl, perhaps siblings, who were so carried away at the sight of a fighter jet that they waved at it in awe. I looked up too, but when I stepped on a couple of corpses, I was reminded again that I was in a race for my life. My eyes welled up with tears. Corpses were littered everywhere. Then I heard a loud chant of "*Nyamiri yakari! O sha baa!*" Not wanting to be discovered, I ran to a tree and stood still until the chant subsided. With my eyes still welled up, I noticed an older woman beckoning at me to come. I wiped my tears to be sure I was seeing a true human.

She persisted. I ran to her, and she guided me to a thatched house. The house was filled with many women. To my utter surprise, my second older sister was there. We screamed but were hushed by the women to be quiet so that we wouldn't be found out. The largest woman in the room asked us to sit on the floor. I was excitedly telling them about how I escaped from a soldier when a rumble of explosions and shelling erupted. I kept quiet. The large woman assured me that I could keep talking but not so loudly. I was about to continue when another shell explosion ripped through the air. This one pierced our roof. It landed on the large woman's left hand. Instantly, a pool of blood settled around her feet. Two women tore off the edges of their wrappers and tied the bleeding hand. The blood gushed. They wrapped the arm firmer and held it up, and the bleeding reduced. That incident was enough to make us decide to find our way to the St. Joseph's women's camp. I clung to my sister even as I whispered all the tales of our mother's worries and how we were not able to find my brother, Big Man. She squeezed my hand and told me that it would be all right, that we would find him. Because we had been in hiding, it was decided that we would find a way to sneak into St. Joseph's because if we were caught as escapees, we might be executed.

We were barely at the St. Joseph's premises when a short, chubby woman called my name. "Are you not Nwasoka Nsugbe?" I didn't say a word. She continued, "They have been dragging your mother and your oldest sister around the whole town threatening to kill them if they don't find you."

A yelp escaped me, but my sister covered my mouth. The lady volunteered to take us to where they were remanded with soldiers watching over them. I hurried to them, but before I could collapse in their arms, three soldiers grabbed me as if I was a wild animal. One slapped me. Another slammed his rifle on my buttocks.

"So you can run," another said. He cupped my breast with a smirk. "You can run with these big things," he said, jiggling them. However, another, a tall, good-looking one, told them to stop. They were surprised at his reaction, and they bragged about how they had had many girls, even those who willingly offered themselves to them to save their families. This good-looking lifesaver asked them to take their hands off me, my sister, and my mother, that he would teach us a lesson himself. He walked us to a deserted area of the premises, and I could hear the screams of young women my age pleading for mercy. Goose bumps spread all over my body, and I remembered why I was bent on escaping. That might be my fate, my sister's, and my mother's.

As he walked us out of St. Joseph campground, another soldier followed him closely. A distance away from the camp, the soldiers that followed us spoke to him in Hausa language. I stared at my oldest sister to see if she could figure out what they were saying. As a teenage bride, she had lived in Kaduna with her late husband. She could understand the language and speak it fluently. But she scowled at me. My mother broke down and pleaded with them to let her see her son before they killed us. My sister acted as an interpreter. Surprisingly, they both said something to each other. The language this time was not Hausa, as my sister confirmed. It was a strange language she couldn't understand.

A few minutes into our walk, a truck full of soldiers stopped right in front of us. A spatter of exchanges in Hausa language ensued. My oldest sister's eyes brightened up. She addressed the soldier holding us captive. Other soldiers hushed her up. My mother warned her not to get us into further trouble. She asked her what they were saying and what she said to them. My oldest sister revealed that the elders of Asaba had called for peace, for an end to the violence. The Nigerian side had invited all men to Ogbe Osowe for peace talks. I could have sworn I saw a smile on my mother's face. She called on Onishe, our river goddess, to save us.

My sister then said that she had asked them to set us free since a peace deal was already in place. But the two soldiers who held us told us to shut up. They took us back to St. Patrick's College. The good-looking soldier said that he had granted my mother's wish to see her son for the last time. My mother and sisters were separated as the soldiers asked me to be the only one to identify my brother. We looked for hours but could not find him. My stomach was growling with hunger, and that was when I realized it was already late in the evening. I begged him to find me something to eat, but he asked me to choose between finding my brother and something to eat.

We were heading to the last building we hadn't searched when I tugged at his hand. I wanted to see how loose his grip was because I was planning another escape in my head. He kicked me, and I shook off the hunger. My brother was in the last building we entered. He was snoozing in a corner. I screamed as soon as I set eyes on him. We hugged and clung to each other before the soldiers separated us. They took us back to where they'd left my mother and my sisters, then headed to one of their bases at Umuagu. They had forcefully taken the Onianwa family home and made it one of their bases. We were shoved into a room and locked up. In there, we lost our sense of time.

***

I was terrified by my mother's story, and I felt "dirty" about being birthed at that time and with an enemy soldier, even though my father saved my mother's family. The war, her story, always made me conflicted, as if there were two people that didn't belong together living inside my being. My parents, a union that morphed into a monster that lived inside of me: a lesbian. I bore my double consciousness like the mark of the beast: a burden I often wished I could strip away. I wanted to be one: one person, from one ethnic group, whole, straight, like everybody else.

3. Reaching

A<small>T</small> U<small>MUNEDE</small>, <small>THE</small> kids I played with were mostly boys. I couldn't relate much to them except that I always wanted to play with them. The oldest of them all was Ezekiel. He was fourteen. I was six. We used to play a horse-riding game. Some of our neighbors would see us playing. They wouldn't say anything, so I thought nothing of it. We took turns to be on our knees like a horse, and then one person would mount and ride away in an imaginary way. But the fourteen-year-old boy would try to poke his penis inside me, and I would ask him to stop. He would stop, but then he would lure me to an isolated storage space a few blocks away from our house. It was where Igbo traders stored their bags of garri. There, he would lift me and place me on top of one of the garri bags and then hump away.

I was perplexed by this because I thought it was part of our horse-ride game. I wondered why it was just me and him when every other game involved about eight of us kids. I did not see anything wrong with the game except for the pain that came with it. But the garri hump became a pattern until I started feeling intense pain in my groin area. I did want to tell my mother at some point that he hurt me when we played, but I didn't want her to stop me from playing entirely.

The last time I remember him taking me to the garri storage place was on a rainy day. On that occasion, the first jab of pain as he tried to thrust his penis inside me sent me into a panic. It felt like my heart was trying to fall out of my chest. He was kneeling, and I was elevated by a garri bag. I reached up and grabbed his short, puffy hair and then screamed with all the strength I could summon. He tried to close my mouth with his right hand as he held onto his turgid penis. I pushed his hand away and screamed even louder. There were sudden voices in the background. He dragged his shorts halfway to his thighs and headed to the open entrance, where he paused with his head cocked to one side as if trying to gauge how close the voices were. I remember the intermittent rain with strong showers rattling through the metal roof. My heart was still thumping, but I made for the door and bolted away. After that, I avoided him. With time, the pain stopped, but I never stopped looking behind me each time I was out playing with other kids.

I became cautious. I would look through our window to see if he was there. Even when he was not, I went out less to play. When I got bored of staying home by myself or watching my mother sew endlessly with her glittery needle and thread, I got a new group of friends. Instead of playing as horses conveying each other from one end of our houses to the other, we invaded the nearby forests, hunting bush rats. Sometimes we ventured into the abysmal Ote forest. We made sure not to stray or be too far apart from one another.

Every rat we caught was skinned, spiced well with salt and pepper and then roasted over the fire we built from broken, dry twigs. We formed a habit of feasting on these, so much so that sometimes when my mother served me a meal, I would refuse. On the days when she was offended by my rejection, she would wave her fingers at me and warn me not to eat in anybody's house because I could be initiated into witchcraft with food and fly at night like bloodsucking bats. Without the blood, I did fantasize some nights about being a bat and flying with reckless abandon. At the first chance I got, I thought, I would suck the life out of Ezekiel until he dropped dead.

One day, I had gathered my hunting friends, anticipating a rich day of rats, only for us to discover that our traps caught nothing. We decided to climb mango and berry trees for some fruit. We'd pluck and eat while lounging on tree branches. We dared each other to play some stunts that included jumping off the tree. Some of the others tried, but I didn't. I imagined what my mother would tell me or do to me if I went home with a broken leg or arm. So I watched as they jumped. While the other kids were carried away in their jumping game, I chitchatted with John. He was my favorite friend because he had a tiny voice and was gentle and kind. He was not rough like the other boys I played with. We decided to hang on to each other while our legs held on to the tree branch for support. We were entangled, swinging back and forth. It was fun, except that I got dizzy at some point.

Out of nowhere, my older brother Dada appeared. He yelled at me and accused me of playing dirty games with boys and ordered me to come down the tree. I was only halfway down when he hauled me over his head and scurried home with me. I was in a panic. I didn't know his intentions, and I didn't want to be thrown down from his wobbly attempt to keep me on his shoulder.

Once home, he told our mother he'd caught me and a boy playing with our private parts entwined. My mother seemed confused. There was a deep furrow between her brows.

My brother was smiling. I was still lost for words. "They were playing dirty games."

I seemed to have found my voice. "We were playing on a tree. We were not playing any dirty game." Before I could finish my words, my mother smacked me across the face.

"Why are you out there with boys? Are you crazy?" She made to hit me a second time, but I ran off. She would always blame me. As a girl, I ought to know better, she would say.

"Come back here, you stubborn child. Come back here, or you will sleep out there on the tree. Stupid!"

My brother didn't need to spring too far before he caught up with me and dragged me back home. As much as I pleaded, he didn't let me go. When he took me to our mother, she already had a whip. She waved it at me and told me she was serving me a warning.

Most of the kids I could find to play with were boys. I hardly found any girls to play with. They were either indoors doing chores or cleaning or doing nothing. How was I to explain that to my mother? I didn't stop playing with boys or anyone who was willing to play with me, but I always made sure my mother was nowhere in sight when I played with them. If anything had gone wrong and my mother got wind of it, it would be my fault. After all, I was the one who "insisted" on playing with them, the one who sought them out. At least, that was the way I interpreted the situation.

4. Branches

U NCLE EMMA WAS a bearded, bulky Igbo man. He lived
two doors away from us, and he owned one of the storage
stores where Ezekiel took me to hump me. As a truck driver and
a businessman, Uncle Emma was gone for weeks on end. He
brought onions and potatoes from the north to sell them to traders
in Umunede. When he came back from his trips, he brought us
treats. We kids always looked forward to his homecoming because
of the many treats he got us. Often, I fantasized that he was my
father, and those warm thoughts of him as my father lifted the
tiny wings in me. He brought out the colors in life, filled me with
the kind of joy that sustained me for days and years. His visits
filled some gaps my father left.

We were in the middle of cooking an imaginary meal one day
when he returned and decided to surprise us. Trying to scare
us, he came at us with a roar. We abandoned our cooking and
scattered around him laughing. He ran, and we chased after him.
The game made us out of breath, but when he saw that we were
getting tired, he slowed down. He scampered to a tree in the
middle of our large compound, grabbed a bag and gave us small
bags of peanuts and cookies. Then he took turns to twirl us in the
air, one after the other.

After the treats, twirls, and hugs, he announced that he was
going to see his wife and kids at Akumazi Umuocha. We yelled
in excitement when he invited us to come with him to visit his
wife and kids, but he warned us not to get too excited because

he needed our parents' permission. I was the first to race to my mother to make the announcement. I proceeded to kneel and beg her to let me go. She ignored me and peeked through the curtain of our window to see what the kids were screaming about. I never knew why she did that because she knew Uncle Emma's voice.

As always, he noticed her at the window and called out her name. "Nwasoka! My sister, how have you been doing? I brought a bag of rice, some onions, and tomatoes for you and the kids."

My mother thanked him profusely.

"It's okay, if that is okay with you. I am taking the other kids too, if their parents allow."

I didn't hear the end of their conversation as I sprang into our bedroom to get my slip-ons.

The trip to Akumazi Umuocha was brief but fun. We would often stop by the roadside to buy roasted corn and the spiced, roasted meat *suya*. Watching bushes and other cars go by was fascinating too. When we stopped to buy snacks, Uncle Emma let us throng behind him to a suya spot where we'd point at the type of meat we wanted. I always wanted chicken gizzard. I liked that it was crunchy. While he haggled with the suya seller, the stench of overflowing gutter and tar would invade my nostrils. I would spit and stare into the night wondering what lurked in the dark as men and women hurried in and out of dimly lit makeshift shacks. There would also be a bunch of women frying eggs and yams by the roadside. There were others frying mackerel fish. The aroma would make my mouth water, but the stench of gutters around us mixed with coal tar made me want to vomit. I would spit endlessly until we left.

The blaring music in the background made the night seem perilous and full of surprises. If it was not a woman chasing after a man for her money, it was a young man making away with a piece of fish displayed for sale. Not too far from us were more men, truck drivers coming in and out of metal sheds with torn curtains and women clinging to their loose wrappers. Some clung close to the men even as the men gave them wads of naira notes. Darkness was not fully descended, but oil lamps made a good light for dimmed transactions.

As we pulled away, munching our meats, the wind blew into our faces, and I clenched even harder on my piece of meat. With every morsel I put into my mouth, I licked my finger. I was not used to so much meat because my mother often rationed what she could share amongst us—herself, my older sister when she was home from boarding school, my older brother, my baby brother, and me.

When we finally arrive at Akumazi Umuocha, Uncle Emma's wife would be as excited as we were to see her husband. She would fuss that it had taken him too long to visit. Then they would turn on the TV for us and head into the bedroom. Our ride back was quieter. Except for chirping crickets and the slight bumps of potholes as we swayed to the movement of the car, we kids were pretty much quiet and sleepy. Uncle Emma was, however, full of stories. I remember asking him why he didn't live with his wife. He said he wanted her to stay in her parents' home since he traveled all the time.

When we got to Umunede, he took each of us home, one after the other, and gave each parent a bunch of bananas and some peanuts. My mother was cradling my brother when she opened the door. She thanked him. When he left, my mother asked me how the trip was. I was sleepy and eager to go to bed. It was good, I said, and slumped on the mattress on the floor.

My brother's cooing sound lingered in the air. I heard my mother's footsteps, the clattering of cups, and breathed in the pleasant aroma of fish subdued by the strong fumes of kerosene. She was cooking. The smell of fish brought back vivid memories of fried mackerel back where we used to live.

I remembered the place. It was a truck stop. Right in front of the building where we lived, Caro fried fish. Her customers came in throngs. Sometimes I helped her stir the wood fire while sparks of flames crackled in the air. Afraid that I might fall into the flames, Caro would get up from her low seat and nudge me away from the fire, and then she would stir more vigorously. The tongues of flames would come alive and lick the bottom of her large frying pan. Before going back to her seat, she would grab a chunk of fish and give me a piece. It was the bounty I often waited around her for. I love food.

While I munched away, I would sit beside her and watch the night. I couldn't understand the hurried steps of truck drivers and the laughter that rang around the frames of women who were led into the night. The place was abuzz with life, and I liked it, in spite of the flames, trucks blaring their horns, and steps I was afraid might crush me. I liked the place until one day, somebody crawled into our house through the window where my cousin Samuel slept.

The room was ransacked and all the newspapers and documents my father kept neatly in the corners were scattered all over the room. We didn't know until my mother's scream tore into the night. There was a man at the top of our window. Perhaps he couldn't get into the second room—our room—through the only door, so he might have decided to climb up our window. My mother's scream frightened me out of sleep. She never stopped screaming even as she clenched her stomach: she was in the ninth month of her pregnancy with my younger brother. I was barely six. She screamed, and all the eaves of our building seemed to be rattling in angst. The climbing thief leaped off the window and fell with a thud. My mother didn't stop screaming until all our neighbors came out. But the thief was gone. However, the chairs and planks he used to climb his way to the window were there. Within a week, my father arranged for us to move to another neighborhood.

I must have fallen asleep because I heard a rooster rousing itself. Then it crowed. I wondered if I had slept at all. It was already morning. A strong waft of my mother's coffee floated across my nose. It smelled nice, but I could never get used to its bitter aftertaste, not even with my expert skills of eating kola nuts. My mother assured me it was an acquired taste, just like the kola nut I shared with my father, and that I would eventually like it.

"Acquire the taste, the way I would acquire my school uniform or my shoes?" I asked. She had promised me new pairs of shoes and uniforms but was yet to buy them.

She laughed and said, "Yes." When she sensed mischief or didn't feel like arguing, she would keep her responses short. I had been badgering her about getting me new pairs of shoes and uniform.

She raised the curtain between the living room and our bedroom, and a sluice of sunlight streamed into the room. I closed my eyes with both of my hands. "Mama, good morning. Can I acquire the taste of your coffee today? I am hungry."

"Good morning, dear. You may finally acquire the taste if you use that chewing stick I gave you and then take a bath."

"Okay, I will." I looked around and there was only my baby brother on the mattress next to me. My older brother was not there. Usually, he slept next to my baby brother. "Where is Dada?"

"He has gone back to school. He left early this morning. Uncle Emma took him to the park."

"Oh!" He didn't even say goodbye.

"You were deep in sleep. I want to go and see our new neighbor and her family. She is from Ibuzo," my mother said.

"Can I come?"

"Not today. Take care of your brother. Next weekend, we can all go and see them."

Thankfully, my baby brother was sleeping, so I swung between daydreaming and snoozing. When my mother came back, she insisted on giving me a bath. She said that I didn't know how to wash myself well, that I was always only scrubbing my belly with the soapy sponge. So I was either wasting her water or only giving my belly a bath.

I didn't like it when she gave me a bath. Her hands were quick and rough, and she scrubbed my skin to the point of almost peeling it off. As if that was not enough, she would chastise me for gathering too much dirt on the soles of my feet. Who washes feet so hard for dirt? When I whined and pouted about how I hated her baths, she would glare at me and tell me that my pouted lips and deep frown made my face look like a pile of shit and would gently splash a handful of water on my face to emphasize her point. For some reason, her splashes of water on my face made me laugh.

As soon as I was dressed, I would be ready to run out and play. I would often forget the "humping" boy until I got to my group of friends. But then, I would turn right around and head home to watch them play from our window. My hunting friends were not always around. I had to seek them out on the days we decided to hunt or check on our traps. The babble and chatter of other kids in my compound made me envious. I would look hard for Ezekiel and sometimes toyed with the idea of running out to play with them if I didn't see him. Oftentimes, I changed my mind. I didn't want to risk it. Maybe he humped other girls like me, but I would count them by their names, and they would all be there playing. Maybe I was the only girl he took to the garri storage space.

Tired of being trapped indoors, it was a relief when my mother took me and my baby brother to see the new neighbor—the lady from Ibuzo. Her name was Angelina Deleke. She had three sons about my age. Their names were Dele, Tunde, and Adebayo. The three boys of the Deleke family were like me and my younger brother. Their father was a Yoruba soldier from Abeokuta. My father was a Tiv soldier from Benue. Their mother was Igbo like my mother, and her town Ibuzo was a twin town to my mother's town, Asaba.

We had not quite sat down when Angelina hurried to the kitchen and came out with a steaming large bowl of jollof rice. She placed it in the middle of a large table in the center of their living room, then rushed back to the kitchen for spoons and plates. My mouth was already watering. She said she needed a big spoon to serve us, but my hand was already reaching out for one of the smaller spoons when I felt my mother's dagger stare on my forehead. I slunk away from the food without trying to meet her gaze and sat back down. She had warned me never to eat at anyone's house except with her permission. If I was already at a friend's house and was invited to eat, how was I supposed to run back home to get her permission before running back to my friend's house to eat? The food would have been finished by then. But nobody questioned my mother.

When Angelina returned with a plate for my mother, she lied. She said we had eaten. I wanted to scream out "No!" but I knew what would await me at home if I embarrassed her in that way. She was quite physically expressive when she wanted to make a point. Angelina insisted, and my mother offered to pray over the food. She served herself a plate and loaded a spoonful into her mouth before she offered me the same plate. She always gave me the impression that if there was witchcraft planted in a food offered to her children, her tasting it first would nullify the potency of the evil placed in the food before she gave it to her children.

5. Sacrificial Calabashes

THE DELEKE BOYS became my new set of playmates, and I introduced them to John. Our trips to the Ote palm plantation were usually happy ones because we caught one or two rats, which we feasted on even if some of us had to make do with the leg or tail. But one of our good hunting days was shattered by a piercing scream from a middle-aged woman. She ran past us sobbing with fitful yelps. There was a trail of people chasing after her until she slumped in the middle of a narrow path.

We followed and joined the crowd that surrounded her, eager to know what was wrong. Her oldest son had beheaded her husband and her younger brother. With the blood-dripping cutlass, the son had jumped into an *omi*, a deep well in the middle of their compound. A woman in an oversized blue blouse narrated as she tried to calm the crying woman.

Some women tried to hold her still as she squirmed and screamed for death to take her too. Some others headed to her house to see if they could save the suicidal son. I was in shock and wanted to go home to my mother, but Adebayo said we should go together to the woman's house to find out if her story was true. I didn't want to, but he pulled me by my hand and jostled toward the thinning crowd. When we got there, the *omi* was surrounded by people peering down the deep well. Even as some old and middle-aged men and women tried to shoo us away from the well, we could see the floating body of the young man. I didn't wait for Adebayo and the rest. I ran.

28

On my sprint home, the sacrificial calabashes that littered the earth paths to my house became more obvious. I slowed down, careful not to step on any. My mother had told me that stepping on one was a bad omen. People used them to cast spells of evil spirits through straying feet. But what could be as bad as what I just witnessed? As I ran home, I shuddered. My mother was at the door when I got home. She was about to leave for an errand. I ran into her and buried my face in her groin.

"What is wrong?" she asked. "Your eyes are as wide as the full moon. Did you run into a boa constrictor?"

I was breathing hard. I couldn't speak. When I finally found my voice, I looked up at her and rattled on incoherently. "Somebody killed everybody in his family including his father. I saw the mother weeping and rolling on the dirt road. When we followed the crowd to see what happened to the man on the killing spree, he had drowned. He jumped into a deep *omi*." I finished and started crying.

My mother wrapped my head with both of her hands and tried to console me. "It's okay. Maybe he ran mad and nobody noticed that something had gone wrong with him."

"You think somebody cast a spell on him and sent an evil spirit to him to kill his family? They used juju on him?"

"Maybe. It could be juju. It could also be that he has madness," she said, still holding my head.

I started throwing a barrage of questions at her. "Do we have madness in our family? Do I have madness? Do you have it?" I had vaguely remembered her telling me and then one of her friends about her late younger brother "Big Man," who was cast with an evil spell, juju, and he had gone mad. He eventually died. My grandmother had resorted to smoking tobacco because of the long, sleepless nights she spent in the shallow room with him at the psychiatric hospital where he was chained.

"What causes madness? Why did he have mental illness?" I wanted to know. My mother guided me to the sofa in our living room and told me that there were many reasons for madness. She would tell me later. She asked me if I wanted to stay with my sleeping brother or come with her to our next-door neighbor to get some salt. Strangely, she seemed unruffled by the incident. Maybe she knew more than she was telling me. I knew that some of our nights were slit with piercing cries of death or violent murder around our neighborhood. Alarmed out of sleep and clutching her bosom, I would ask her why such piercing screams tore through some nights. She would sigh and tell me we would never know why certain things happen. The eeriness of Umunede stayed with me long after we left it.

Afraid to be home alone with my brother, I followed her. We met Papa Ikpeamanam in the common corridor we shared with him. He was locking his door and gleaming with the brightness of his white shorts. He strutted forward, ahead of us. I admired his well-ironed security uniform. Short and dark, he could almost pass for a little person; he was almost the same height as me, just a few inches taller. He seemed even stranger to me whenever he rolled a massive ball of fufu, dipped it into his watery soup and swallowed. The ball of fufu was always as massive as my head, and I never stopped wondering how he pushed it through his tiny throat.

He had two grown sons and a very pretty daughter who was the color of a pale sun. Her smile was even more beautiful; it seemed to burst open like a blooming flower whenever I gazed at her. There was something disarming about her high cheekbones and mustard skin. Her name was Adaafor. I always found myself staring at her. It became a habit, and when she touched me, it felt like a healing balm. Suddenly, one day, she disappeared. My mother said that her father had married her off. I did overhear some of our neighbors say that her father was pressed for money so he married her off to a man with a hunchback. I was trailing my mother, deep in thought about Adaafor, when she shouted at me to quicken my steps.

When we got to Mama Eke's door—one of our neighbors—we knocked, and the door swung open. She was standing there squinting her eyes. My mother apologized for waking her up.

"Miss," she addressed my mother. Most people addressed my mother as Miss, even my older sister, because my mother was considered a young, classy teacher.

"Good day," she said.

I mumbled "hello" and stepped behind my mother to hide from Mama Eke. She had a habit of pulling my ears as a way of saying hello to me.

My mother thanked her for the salt. We hurried home. My brother was still asleep when we got home. With her nose in the air, my mother sniffed and said that he must have soiled the small towel she used on him as diapers. She gently turned him around and unwrapped his wadded buttocks. Before she could completely unwrap the whole cloth, he woke up and started crying. She thrust her left breast into his mouth and continued cleaning him. When she was done, we sat on the sofa, quiet. A light thunder cackled in the distance. After a while, I asked her to tell me a story.

She told me a story about the tortoise and the birds.

There was famine in the land, and only the birds had food because they could fly to different places to find it. One day, while they were feasting, Tortoise crawled up to them to beg for food. They scoffed at him and asked him what gave him the nerve to come to them for food. They told him to look at them and to look at himself; they had nothing in common. They further asked him why they should give him food when he had nothing to offer then in return.

Tortoise told them that even though they laughed at him for crawling instead of flying like they did, they all shared the same animal kingdom and they never knew when they might need him. They flapped their wings even more vigorously and laughed even harder. Then they continued with their feast and ignored the tortoise. He watched them from a corner as they gobbled up loads of food and wine.

As pangs of hunger hammered him harder, he picked up the courage and crawled back to them. They warned him to keep away, but one of the red birds picked a bone from the pile of their leftover trash and tossed it at him. Tortoise caught it midair and scraped out and ate some bits and pieces of meat from the bone. They kept tossing all the bones at him. He gathered all the bones and was able to have a meal from the small bits of flesh stuck on the bones. When he was full, he left. The birds didn't even know when he left.

After a few years, some strange flying animals appeared in the kingdom. They were attacking birds for no reason, so the birds were taking shelter in caves and at the foot of mountains. Yet these strange animals with long noses found the birds and killed them.

"Why were their noses long?" I interjected.

"So they could sniff out the birds."

One day, as the tortoise was walking home from a stream where he had gone to drink some water, he saw the strange flying animal aiming for a red bird in flight. The bird knew that he would not be able to escape the animal. It was too fast. He flew toward the tortoise, who raised his shell and pushed the bird under him. The strange flying animal tapped his nose on the tortoise's shell to bite him, but the shell was too hard. It flew away. That was how the bird was saved.

"But why did the tortoise help the bird when it didn't even want to give him any food?" I asked.

"I guess the tortoise is a forgiving and kind person."

"If I were the tortoise, I wouldn't help him. The bird even made a mockery of him as a crawling animal."

"I know, but he is a kind person."

"Why does he have to be kind by not punishing the bird? He should have punished the bird for being mean to him."

"Well, dear, as they say, two wrongs do not make a right."

6. In Flight

THAT NIGHT, I became both a bird and a tortoise. At first, I was a tortoise and burrowed my way through all types of tunnels and stumbled upon lakes and seas. I swam with the fish and lay in fields. Next, I became a bird and flew across seas and oceans. I saw different places and huge forests. I perched on shrubs to eat fruit and insects. I was free to roam, but I enjoyed wading in large bodies of water the most.

My mother's firm hands woke me as she lifted and guided me to the mattress where I slept. I was a bit disappointed. The dream seemed real. For a few minutes before I fell asleep, I thought I heard somebody knocking on the door and telling my mother that he had a letter for her. Sleep was overpowering me. I tried to listen but heard only chirruping crickets and scurrying rats. Then it sounded as if pebbles were dropping on our zinc roof. Even as the pounding of the rain gathered strength, I thought I heard my mother crying.

"Mama!" I called out.

"It's okay, dear. Get some sleep."

For some reason, fear enveloped me. I had never heard my mother cry even when she talked about her younger brother, Big Man. The last time, I heard her choke in tears when she told me how smart her brother was. He'd even earned a scholarship to study in the United Kingdom. She said he often wrote their mother to complain about how a black cat troubled him every night. It would perch on his windowsill and invade his thoughts for nights on end.

Big Man barely gave them enough time to process the mysterious development before he returned to Nigeria, deranged. She told me that those periods started my grandmother's nightmare of clanking chains and the hideous roars of her last son and child. His transformation kept her up all night. She prayed to our river goddess, Onishe, to intervene and to ease her mind in the chaos that had become her life. Relentlessly, she resorted to snorting and smoking tobacco. The memories of my mother recounting the stories about her brother and my grandmother's experiences flooded my mind. I sighed to fight back tears. I lulled between sleep and wakefulness.

That night, I felt a distance sit between me and my mother like a deep gully. I wanted to get up and go to her, tell her that everything would be all right. I couldn't get up. I wanted to call out to her, but I couldn't speak. For some reason, I had lost my voice. I started thinking about some of our days in the past, the days we danced to Boney M's "Baby Do You Want To Bump." I remember troughs of sunlight lit up the room. I screeched to the bump and beat of the song, hopping from my right leg to my left. My mother would tell me to give her room to show me how it was done. She would wriggle her behind, and we would simultaneously scream. We were determined to out-dance each other. Drafts of her coffee floating in every space made the dance contest more exciting. Now everything seemed to have changed. The sound of raindrops lulled me to sleep.

The next day, as were the rest of the weeks, there were more whispers in the house. Angelina visited my mother more, and we never went to her after our first couple of visits. The air of silence settled on our house like a suffocating blanket. My mother started wearing only black clothes. She became sad and droopy and yelled more. Nobody told me anything, but I noticed the change. She wore a black dress for a long time. Within a few weeks, before I could ask any questions, she bundled us to Asaba to live with my grandmother.

My grandmother was almost eighty, but she was still very strong and fleet-footed. She was the one who told me that my father had died in a car accident. That day, she and my mother hurried us to a medicine woman's house near the river Niger. They had taken us there for herbal blade incisions to keep my father's ghost away. When I asked why, she told me that the dead linger in the land of the living because they need to be cleansed of their worldly ills before they are allowed to join the land of the spirits. My father had gone out with his friends, but his friends got drunk and ran into a stationary truck on the side of the road. Neither he nor his friends survived the accident. Where my mother said very few words, my grandmother never kept any secrets from me.

Between raising her chickens in a small room next to where we slept, she also sold little snacks for our upkeep. At night, she never failed to tell me stories about tortoises and their smart and cunning ways. My grandmother didn't have much, but she fed me with unlimited stories, and I began to create some of these stories in my head, especially when she was too tired or too busy to tell me more. Though she didn't have much, she fed us as well as she could. Sometimes, she would use onions and fresh vegetables to make an old pot of soup come alive. Sometimes, we ate the same soup three times a day. On the mornings she couldn't scrape up anything, she would give us slices of dry bread with tea. It was one of those mornings, on my way to school, that I walked past a trash dump and saw some oranges. They looked fresh. I walked into the dump and picked up two halves, wiped the surface with the back of my hand and ate them. It was filling.

At school, I was not doing so well. Some of my teachers were my mother's friends and schoolmates from when she was at the teachers' training college. They would often wonder why I was dull, unlike my mother who they said was very intelligent. It was then I met Ms. Onwubiko. Her smile was what mostly kept me captivated by her presence. She was my English and literature teacher. Whenever she spoke to me, it made my day, and I started following her around like a puppy. She didn't seem to mind.

One day, she pulled me aside to ask me if everything was all right at home. I was excited about her interest in my life outside of class. I told her that I lived with my grandmother and that my parents did not live at Asaba. She smiled that wonderful smile and gave me a hug. Her embrace felt so good I didn't want to let go. She gently disentangled herself from me.

In the subsequent weeks, she consistently brought me snacks, mostly mangoes and oranges, but after a while, she stopped, and the attention she gave me began to wane. Whenever I met her, she'd tell me to go to my seat and sit down. When I saw her and scuttled up to greet her in hope for another hug, she merely waved at me and asked how I was doing. So many times, I rehearsed walking up to her and asking her why she'd changed, but I couldn't summon up the courage. I had another idea though.

On a hot Tuesday morning, she took us out to the wide school field for physical activity. We were to sprint. After the warm-up, she took a long rope, set it down in the center of the field, and then asked all of us to line up. She wanted to make sure we were in a straight line before she placed her whistle on the tip of her lips.

"On your marks!"

"Wait!" I yelled and walked up to her. "I want to remove my sandals first!"

"Okay," she said, smiling into my face. That warmed my heart.

"I am ready," I told her.

"Good!"

"On your marks. Set. Go!"

I shot right ahead of my classmates, but halfway along the field, I observed that most of them were already ahead of me. I didn't want to disappoint her. I also thought it was a good opportunity to get her attention. I fell and faked a faint. The sprint was already over when some classmates gathered around me, yelling that I had passed out. Within minutes, Ms. Onwubiko was by my side. She asked students to move away so I could get some air. She cradled me in her arms and kept calling my name in a low voice. I didn't as much as move a limb. Then she asked one of the students to run and get some water.

With some sprinkles of water on my face, I involuntarily gasped. She scattered more on my face. Some trickled down my chin. I opened my eyes. She asked me if I could walk and then tried to lift me. I got up, and she guided me back to the class and brought me some cookies and a bottle of Fanta. When I was done eating, she asked me if I wanted to go home and rest, or if I wanted her to let the headmistress know if they should send for my grandmother or take me to the hospital. I told her that I was okay, that the Fanta and cookie had given me some energy.

After that incident, she paid more attention to me by often asking how I was doing and if I had eaten. I enjoyed this very much. It warmed up a part of my body that was neither my belly nor my heart. I was drawn to her the way I was drawn to my mother. She was tough and yet had a soft side. That relationship didn't have a chance to grow because a few days later, my mother pulled me and my brother back to Umunede. My grandmother had been hit by a car.

My grandmother had a schedule of going to the market in the late evening when fish sellers had become desperate to sell the last bits of fish they had. It was cheap then. That day, she had grabbed her basket, tied her scarf firmly around her head and strutted to the market right across from our house, the Nsugbe's compound, at Nnebisi Road. She had dashed across the busy road and hadn't seen the car racing toward her at full speed. She was knocked down and out. Earlier, she had told me to gather the wood so that she would make a fire and cook our dinner when she got back from the market. We had a routine of eating fresh fish soup with pounded yam or fufu. She always made sure we had a treat of meat or a piece of fish whenever she cooked because for me and my brother a meal was not complete without a piece of fish or meat.

I was still gathering the wood, distracted by the tiny beetles that were crawling out of the wood, when one of our neighbors told me that my grandmother had been taken to the hospital because a car had knocked her down. It took me a while to understand what she meant. I had just seen my grandmother and we were going to have our usual *nsala* soup. The neighbor didn't wait for me to respond and concluded by saying my aunt was going to take care of me and my younger brother.

On the day my mother appeared, even though I was sad and worried about my grandmother, my mother's presence felt as if heaven had burst open to swallow me in a rapture. As soon as I saw her come around the only bend to our enclosed compound, I flew into her arms and yelled, "Mama!" I held her tight, not wanting to let her go for fear that she might leave again without me. She held on to me for as long as I held her.

Eventually, she said, "Let go, dear. We could be here holding on to each other until dawn breaks. I am happy to see you too."

"What happened to Nne?" I asked, which was what we called my grandmother.

"She will be okay. She is in the hospital."

"What happened?" I insisted.

My mother shoved some peanuts and bananas into my hands without saying a word. I looked up at her, eager for some answers. "She will be fine."

It was not until a few hours later when my mother got back from visiting my grandmother that I overheard her telling our neighbor that my grandmother had suffered a concussion and that her jaw was broken. Until then, I hadn't realized how serious her condition was. A dreary air hung in our home.

My uncle's visit changed everything. Amid apprehension and fright, there were smiles and cheerfulness. He looked like my mother except that he smiled more and he had no hair on his head. In fact, his head shone like the surface of a well-polished glass. So when he looked at me one Sunday afternoon, I saw my mother's face. She had overwhelmed me with stories of her older brother, Odimma.

He had raised her as a young teen, especially when she lived with him in Port Harcourt, and he had encouraged her to continue school by enrolling her at Ovim Girls' School in Imo state. His passion for education came early, my mother told me. He was so smart when he was in high school he was tagged "Electric Brain," so it was no surprise to my mother and their other siblings when he got a full scholarship to study in the United Kingdom. My uncle's visit was to take my grandmother with him to the University of Nigeria medical hospital at Nsukka. That also meant that my mother took me and my younger brother back with her. This time, she was posted to a remote village, Azagba near Idu, for teaching.

39

7. Sprouts

WHEN MY MOTHER told me I would be spending a good part of the vacation with her at Idu, I was so thrilled that the drudgery of chores—cooking, washing, and sweeping—disappeared. I gave a tune to every chore. I dished out food generously and even discovered a new way of killing flies. Instead of the brutal way of smashing them into pulp with a broom, I peppered them with kerosene.

She had told me a tale about the town where her school was located. Idu village was reputed to have made a ghost god. Their oracle had demanded that if they wanted a good supply of water, they should bury an albino named Idu alive. But the spirit of the albino refused to rest and roamed around the area where he was buried. I laughed at this strange tale. Until I heard her say that it was the village where her school was located, I never knew that such a place existed. As my day of departure drew closer, I stayed awake into the nights thinking about what it would be like to be a teacher's daughter in a village. I knew I had to polish my spoken English to impress the village students.

When we arrived, my mother said that she hoped I would enjoy my stay there. "There are quite a lot of children your age in my new school. I am sure you'll make lots of friends before your vacation ends."

I saw the village of Idu with a new pair of eyes on the day I arrived. Everything seemed conspicuous. There were many trees and bushes, and the path we walked was dusty. There were no paved roads; the footpaths wound around mud huts. As we walked past a cluster of mud houses, many large-eyed children gazed at me. Some were half-dressed, some naked. We came to a bigger path and saw some men, women, and children sitting on an enormous log surrounded by piles of yams. Chickens and tethered goats wandered about.

It looked like the village market. Some women traders, young men, and girls stood around. One of the women had the end of her left breast in her baby's mouth while she rummaged in a basket beside her. Another woman clutched a hen under her arm. A tall man with sunken cheeks emptied a generous amount of ground tobacco into his right nostril with his thumbnail. He pressed the other nostril with his finger and inhaled deeply. Then he sneezed violently, blowing out brown mucus. When he cleared his throat, his gaunt cheeks seemed to deepen. The rest of the people looked out expectantly at the empty road.

"What are they waiting for?" I asked my mother.

"They are waiting for the next bus to take them to Muje, seven miles away. Today is their market day."

We walked on without looking back until we got to the place she shared with some of her fellow teachers, who were also her friends. It was one of the few cement houses with zinc roofs, quite unlike Asaba. Most of the houses in Asaba were cement houses. As soon as we entered the compound, she yelled out, "We're here! Who is home?"

"We're home!" a voice shrieked. Three women ran out and nearly pushed us down in greeting. The tallest of the three hugged me. As I looked up to see her face better, the sun hurt my eyes. She had a long face with small eyes and a nose like a bird's beak. Her hair was braided backward into four rows. She had only one cowry earring on her right ear.

"Why the frown?" she asked, taking my metal box.

"Oh, nothing, it's the sun!" I responded and squinted my eyes.

The second woman, who was short and fair in complexion, shook my hand and grinned at me. The third, rather lean, with thick locks of hair hanging down to her shoulders, held my hand and looked intently at me. I stared at the ground, twisting the hem of my dress. My grandmother had told me that some women with thick locks dashed with cowries were the priestesses of Onishe, our river goddess. I wondered what she was doing in my mother's house; she should be at the shrine of the goddess.

"You're such a beauty!" she exclaimed, letting go of my hand.

"Yes!" my mother interrupted. "Doesn't she look just like me?" She introduced the woman as Kachi. The tall one was Ama; the other, Sinke.

My mother's sitting room was sizable, with three chairs and a low table in the middle, and in a corner, a chair and a big table with some books neatly arranged on it. While the ladies sat down, my mother took me to her bedroom next to the sitting room. The room was untidy. There were four combs, two of which had hairs stuck between their teeth. There were also used chewing sticks, broken pencils, and a tattered bible. Her cooking pots were scattered on the floor. Her two suitcases, one on top of the other, had some of her clothes sticking out.

I hissed at the sight of these. If this were my room, she would not have let me keep it as untidy. As soon as she asked me to change clothes and set my box on the floor, I gathered the pots into a corner of the room, piled all the combs, pencils and chewing sticks in one corner of the windowsill, changed into a casual dress, and pushed my box under her wooden bed. By the time I got back to the sitting room, a steamy plate of okra soup and pounded cassava, *akpu*, was waiting for me. The ladies invited me to eat. As I rolled my first lump of fufu, Kachi poured out some water for me.

"What class are you in?" she asked.

"I am supposed to have finished my primary school, but I am repeating primary five, though I took the common entrance examination. I am waiting for the results to be released," I answered and swallowed my third lump of fufu.

"Would you like to come here for your secondary school?" Sinke asked.

"No, this place is just a village."

Kachi and Sinke looked at each other and roared with laughter. I stopped rolling the next lump of fufu, wondering why they were laughing.

"So we are villagers. We're not fancy enough for you!" Sinke cut in.

"No, that is not what I mean..." I said, but their laughter drowned out my explanation.

"Would you prefer to live in a boarding house or...?" Ama did not finish her question before my mother interrupted her.

"Let her be, you will make her choke. Be patient, she will have plenty of time to answer all your questions."

They apologized and kept quiet while I finished my food. Ama washed my plate, and Sinke took a bucket full of water to the bathroom for me. Kachi volunteered to bathe me.

"She is a big girl. She will not accept that favor!" my mother cut in, smiling broadly.

I was still asleep when my mother was getting ready to go to her school the next morning, but she woke me as she tried to pull the blanket over my legs. I opened my eyes, mumbling a good morning. She was all dressed up and looking down at me. I leaped out of bed and pleaded with her to wait for me while I took a quick bath. When I realized that I had to wait for one of her neighbors who was in the bathroom to come out, I merely used a piece of cloth and dry-cleaned my body. My mother noticed and insisted I should take a real bath, so as not to give her students a bad first impression about me. I waited until her neighbor came out of the bathroom and took a rushed bath, then dressed up.

The walk to school was not long, and the cool morning air felt nice. Except for looking back a number of times to ask me to walk faster, my mother did not say much until we got to her school. It was very small: two blocks of long buildings with a rusty zinc roof. Some parts of the roof were torn off and flapping in the wind. The two buildings had no classrooms in them, just a huge hall; each class had its own corner in the hall. The noise from each section disturbed the other classes. My school at home was far better than this.

My mother introduced me to some of her colleagues. They shook my hand and offered me oranges and cookies. Then she asked some of her students to keep me company while she prepared her lesson notes. Some of the students came and crowded around me. I pulled away from them, but they followed me to a shady spot under a baobab tree. Some of them reached out and touched me.

"What is your name?" they chorused.

"Unoma," I answered. I was beginning to enjoy the attention. I felt like a queen attending to her subjects.

"Is your place like our place?" one of them asked.

"No, you have a lot of bush here."

There was a pause. Many of them merely stared at me. The one I noticed the most was a girl with a dimple. Her eyes were large too. She introduced herself as Isioma. I liked her instantly and moved closer to her. She kept pulling at the brown leather belt around my dress. I would pull away and then tug at her hand. We would both giggle. When she pulled at it a second time, I pulled her left ear and ran. She chased after me. I had hoped she would chase me alone, but the whole crowd of students raced after me. This caught my mother's attention, and she yelled at us to be calm.

We fell quiet, then I led Isioma away from the crowd to another shaded tree. We sat there and talked as if we had been friends for a long time. She was her parents' only child. She said her parents didn't let her have many friends so she was excited to be my friend. I told her I would love to be her friend too. There was a moment of silence. As I looked at her, I was taken in by her dimple. I drew closer to her and kissed her cheek. She giggled and kissed me back on my cheek. We laughed again, and I hugged her tight. We clung to each other until I saw my mother at a distance looking around, and I just knew she was looking for me. I disentangled myself from pretty Isioma, took her hand, and hurried toward my mother. My mother took my hand and asked Isioma to go to her class because recess was over. Before she ran off, she promised to come and look for me in my mother's class.

At second recess, they gathered around me again. I felt like an exotic bird chirping away while they watched. Isioma was standing next to me and we leaned on each other. Then I addressed the crowd of students: "What would you like to do at the university when you leave here?"

They stared at me.

"University?" one of them asked.

Others yelled out, "Lawyer!" "Nurse!" "Mechanic!" "Teacher!" "Doctor!" "Farmer!" "Tailor!"

When their yelling died down, I explained to them that the words "mechanic," "farmer," and "tailor" were not good words, that mechanics should be called mechanical engineers, farmers should be called agriculturalists, and tailors, fashion designers. They roared in laughter, shooting their hands into the air.

When they became quiet, another asked me, "What about you? What would you like to become when you grow up?"

"I would like to study sociology or psychology at the university."

One of them whistled and hopped around, chanting "Logy! Logy!" The rest of them joined in the chant.

My mother must have heard the shout and cheers because she looked out through the window, and I saw what looked like worry in her eyes.

"He-iiii!" she yelled. "Keep it down. Don't suffocate her. Give her some space to breathe."

I stood on my toes and craned my neck to make her see me above the students.

"Mama, it's okay. They were only listening to my story!"

"I see...but sit down, all of you, give her some air!"

Before they could all sit down, the end-of-recess bell rang. They cried in disappointment and dispersed, but Isioma lingered and hugged me again. I kissed her dimpled cheeks and she ran off in a titter.

8. Loose Roots

As DAYS AND weeks went by, I continued to teach them more words. It became something we did nearly every day. This earned me the name "Unono logy." Everywhere I went, I was hailed as "Unono logy," even in the market. I became very popular. When my mother asked me the origin of the name, I explained it to her. She laughed and suggested that I should teach them a new set of career choice names. I did. My crowd of admirers increased, and I started thinking of what to tell my mother to make her let me stay with her. I was becoming fond of Isioma, and I didn't want to leave the village anymore. But the village had one major problem: no running water. Students helped my mother fetch water from a distant stream.

As their vacation approached, my mother instructed me to start fetching water with them. They were doing it without me before, but she felt it was important that I joined them because their parents might complain if it became an everyday task they performed for her. I panicked. I didn't want Isioma to see me fetching water with a clay pot or bucket on my head. I was uncomfortable with the idea because the status I had gained might diminish. I was already very close to Isioma. The tree behind my mother's house was our favorite place to tell stories, play, hug, and kiss. That had become our ritual, and I wanted her admiration of me to stay the same. My mother tried to work against me by insisting that I should fetch water with them.

On the first day my mother asked me to join them, I told her I had a headache. She gave me some painkilling tablets. The second time, I told her I was not feeling so well. I did not know that she had collected some herbs for fever and cooked them for me. When she brought a cupful, I was surprised and told her I had recovered. She did not believe me, but I managed to convince her. I hated those herbs; they were worse than bitter leaves. But my tricks were running out. If I did not come up with something more convincing next time, my mother would know I was avoiding going to the stream with the students.

The next day, I had just finished eating and was waiting for Isioma and throwing pebbles at some birds in front of the house when my mother called my name. I guessed she was calling me to join the students to fetch water. I called out that I was coming but ran into the toilet. I came out and told her I had a dysentery. She smacked me at the back of my neck and shouted at me to get the bucket from the kitchen. Isioma was right there. She stood like a statue, and I felt so ashamed of myself. My mother kept shouting that my grandmother had spoiled me rotten and that she was going to take me back to her so that she could finish what she started with me. "Go into that kitchen before I get you a cane as tall as you are!"

I tore into the house trying to avoid Isioma's eyes, but she came after me and tried to console me.

"I'll go with you to the stream. It's okay. We can swim there together."

I felt better when she kept holding me and telling me it was okay. But there was still some shame threatening to bring me to the brink of tears. I held it back.

Going to the stream gave us more time together. Even though I knew my mother would be checking her clock to know when we'd get back, Isioma's dimpled smiles kept me enthralled. Her gentle and caring nature soothed me. We progressed from hugging and kissing on the cheeks to kissing on the mouth. Each time we kissed we giggled. Scrambling through bushes and chasing after each other consumed our time, but we eventually made it to the stream. With large swaying pots of water on our heads, there was not much we could do without risking tripping and breaking the pots. So we just sang or told stories until we got to my mother, who would look at her watch and tell us that if we continued at the pace we were, we would not achieve much. We resorted to running to see who got there first.

Our happy days drew to a close on the day my mother declared that my holiday with her was over. My school at Asaba was about to start for the new term. I was devastated. I had forgotten all about Asaba. I begged my mother to let me live with her. She refused. I cried and told her that something terrible could happen to me at Asaba. She shook her head and told me what day I would leave. I didn't want to tell Isioma. I didn't want to cry and I didn't want her to see me cry. I left without saying a word.

I was hurt the most when my mother was transferred back to Umunede before she completed a full year at Idu primary school. I was moving again, dizzy from being tossed between my mother and my grandmother and when I'd found a friend I had a strong connection with. I left Idu with a broken heart. Something in me broke. Its pieces eventually became the shards of me I had to contain. I had to gather the edges of my pain to keep from bleeding out.

My mother's return to Umunede was the return for my younger brother and me as well. Umunede remained the same as before except that my mother met a new family from Ibuzo. At first, I didn't understand the relationship. The man and his wife had five sons, and one of them, Ifeanyi, was about my age. Often, we would leave their place and go to ours to play house. The game was okay when I was supposed to be the mommy and cook for our kids. However, when Ifeanyi started humping me, I protested and asked that we take turns to hump each other. He insisted that only daddies humped. I insisted that we'd take turns to hump each other, but the game ended when we never agreed on equal humps. I told him that he was no longer welcome to be one of the group of friends who went rat hunting or played soccer with me sometimes.

Then my mother started having arguments with his mother. I think Ifeanyi's father wanted my mother to be his second wife, but Ifeanyi's mother was not happy about it. I was not sure what the conflict was about, but I had overheard some of my mother's friends tell her she needed a man, even if the man was married, to help her take care of her children.

It was not too long after my mother had exchanged words with Ifeanyi's mother, we started seeing strange objects in front of our house, from dead birds to dead cats to sacrificial calabashes. Then she would take me with her to drop her own sacrificial objects at the crossroad leading to Ifeanyi's house. But our midnight trips to the crossroad came to a sudden halt. My mother ended her relationship with Ifeanyi's father and started a prayer session with a high, yellow, well-shaven prophet. We were there every night at his altar where he would have us kneel, and then he would pray above us. When he was done, he made the sign of the cross on our foreheads with what he called anointed oil. The part of the prayer routine that I liked was the walk to the prophet's house.

The night, the stars…felt liberating. There were night traders calling out their wares for sale. Cars and trucks blared their horns, creating an exciting buzz of sound and light. The shadows of the night were often broken by slanted headlights of trucks heading north. The wind washing my face was relaxing. These lively moments slowed down my pace as I longed to merge with the night and settle at a tranquil place in the midst of scattered chaos. Then my mother would look back and ask me to hasten my steps. Shadows wrapped me in safe spaces. Between skips and short runs, we matched our mother's steps. When my little brother whined in tiredness, she gathered him into her arms. The night tarried as we disappeared into the bend that led to the prophet's home and altar.

In school, I was not reading as well as I wanted to. I had watched my classmates read with such speed. I still struggled with pronouncing some words and I could not read as fast as some of them. Most of the teachers and students knew my mother as the English and home economics teacher. She started reading bedtime stories to me every night, introducing me to more words and then teaching me how to pronounce the words I struggled with. She read to me in English but it sparked a fire from where my grandmother left off in her indigenous tales. The stories my mother read to me, just like the ones my grandmother told me, seemed to be in faraway places, except that the pictures in the books my mother read to me had pale-looking people. They spoke of snow and summer. She had to explain the seasons to me. Winter was like our harmattan when everything was cold with dry air. The spring and summer were like our rainy season when everything is warm and wet.

With time, I could read and write at a pace I liked, and I volunteered to read in class at every opportunity I could get. I stopped depending on my mother to read books and stories. I started writing my own. However, most of my writings were more questions than coherent narrative. I started with short lines and verses. Our reading routine was broken when we had to return to Asaba again. This time, it was in 1979.

My mother could not afford to rent a house, but her older brother's building was vacant at Asaba. She asked to move into the building and we did. He had given her a timeframe to move out because he wanted to renovate the house. My mother agreed. I was re-enrolled in the same school I had left a couple of years ago, but it didn't feel the same. My favorite teacher was no longer teaching there. Often, I would daydream or stand aloof.

That period ended quickly because my grandmother had returned and she found ways to make my world eventful. She looked refreshed and her fair skin glowed, but her jaw seemed to have shifted slightly to the left. That didn't affect her radiant smile though. I had a million questions for her about what happened when she had the accident. Patiently, she told me about her experience at Nsukka. She slept more, and whenever she dozed off in the middle of telling me a story, I would sneak off to our neighbors to play soccer with some of the boys that lived close to our neighborhood, including my cousins. My mother would often find me at makeshift football pitches.

Once, she appeared earlier than I had expected. We hadn't even completed the first half when her voice pierced through that moment of joy, when I was so sure I would have scored that one goal if she hadn't startled me. She wanted me to stop playing soccer with the boys. Instead, I was to hasten to the kitchen, wash the dishes and tidy up. I was so mad. I dared to question her. I asked her why I was always the one being constantly called upon to do chores, to cook, to clean, and wash dishes, but none of that for my brothers.

I can't quite express the shock on my mother's face after I asked her the question. I had always been the good, obedient little girl. Then she spat these words at me: "How dare you question me? Who will take care of your husband and your children when you get to your husband's house? Will your brothers help you when you get to your husband's house?"

My response was: "I don't want any of that. I don't want to be anybody's slave!"

That shocked her even more. She didn't need to waste any more words. Instead, she dashed toward me, and I tore into the wildest race of my life. I believed that the kind of wrath my comment had stirred up in her was enough to make her beat me to a pulp if she had caught me. So, I ran.

It was at that age I think I became more assertive. I also observed that my mother was quick to yell at me for something I did wrong. It was either that I sat with my legs wide open or I was a little too aggressive because I played soccer with boys. She would chastise me for not knowing my place. I remember her lunging at me, hitting me, when I refused to hug a guest who wanted to compliment me for my good grades in school. I did thank him, but I refused his hug. It was not merely the brown patches of sweat around the armpits of his gray shirt that annoyed me; it was his eyes, too, the way they hovered around my sprouts of breasts.

I was always at loggerheads with my mother. I disliked domestic chores. I hated dresses. I would rather climb trees and challenge boys. My mother watched all these, hell-bent on setting me straight before the larger world sank its teeth into me. Try, she did. She was always either chasing after me or jabbing her chubby hands under the bed to reach me where I hid. I was neither her first daughter nor her last child, but between the two of us, we kept each other busy.

I seemed to sober up when I started menstruating. I was afraid to tell her about the blood trickling down my legs. "She will kill me!" I muttered to myself. "She will say I did something wrong." Terrified, I ran into the room I shared with my brother and locked the door. I scrambled around for an old dress, and then shoved it between my legs. My heart was beating fast. There was nobody I could talk to. I couldn't talk to my older sister. After the long years she'd spent in a boarding school, we seemed to have grown distant from each other. Besides, she hated my guts, and she was everything I didn't want to be. Obsessed with marriage and motherhood, she taunted me about how I would never find a man to marry me. What could be worse than not finding a man to marry? With a rag well wedged between the crevices of my pelvic area, I cried myself to sleep.

A loud knock made me scramble to my feet. I ran to the door without realizing the rag between my legs had fallen off. My mother had followed a line of ants to my room. The ants had found a piece of candy I had hidden away from my brother; I had forgotten all about it. She followed it to where I had wrapped it in one of my dresses. But then her eyes caught sight of my blood-stained dress. She ignored the trail of ants and faced me. I kneeled and begged her not to beat me. I tried to tell her I didn't know what had happened.

To my shock, she gathered me into her arms and said, "My little girl has become a woman," ruffling my hair before reaching out for another old cloth. She ripped a rope out of it, wrapped up the remaining piece, and tied the rope around my thighs while my small frame trembled. She strapped the rag around the rope and between my legs. I looked into her eyes for an explanation, but there was no expression on her face. All she said was, "Now you must really stop playing with boys!"

9. Nsukka Hills Like Wombs

SOON WE WERE headed to Nsukka. It was me, my younger brother, and my cousin D. The ride was long but the crooning voices of Skyy's "Call Me" kept us busy as we swayed to every song on the album. The vanilla air freshener and the smell of fresh leather in a brand-new car stuck in my nose until we got to Nsukka.

It was evening when we arrived. My cousins—my uncle's younger kids—were on their bicycles and had stopped to welcome us. I had asked one of them if I could ride their bicycle. The last time I rode one was when my older sister's boyfriend let me ride his. It was not an entirely great experience because the pole across the bicycle kept hitting my vulva, so I figured out a way to ride it without hurting myself. I rode sideways so a part of my thigh was on the pole. After a brief bicycle ride, we were taken to our room. It was what used to be my uncle's study.

Being with my uncle, his wife, and my cousins made me think about my older siblings. My cousins' presence made the reality of my older siblings' tangible. I realized that whatever memories I held of them often receded to the background because we were not really close. It was not their fault. It was mostly because I noticed early in life that I was different, and my being different made me lonely. So I was very much aware of my loneliness in spite of their presence. I wondered if that was going to be my fate with my cousins, especially because with them, there was already a difference. I felt as if we were at their mercy, as they had been gracious enough to take us in to ease the burden for our single mother. I did wonder if we were to show our gratitude in ways that might be expected of "rescued" children.

In no time, we were enrolled at the University of Nigeria primary school where my cousins attended school too. But for me, my brother, and D, our routine at home was established. We woke up early, at about five a.m., and stacked up firewood to build a fire for hot water for everyone to use. Nsukka was rather cold. After our baths, we would quickly complete our chores, which included sweeping the sizable compound and cleaning out the kitchen. Then we would rush breakfast and get ready for school. Often, we tried to hurry with our chores so that we could all go together with my cousins.

In some cases, when I was late to join the driver and my cousins, I had to run to school, which was quite some distance. I didn't mind that. I had the chance to feel the wind on my face. What hurt me were occasional days when we ran out of tomato stew. I had to eat my yam with palm oil. The pain was not because I didn't have at least a little bit of the delicious stew, it was because I didn't have any meat. When my grandmother gave me yam and palm oil, she would always give me an egg or break out a piece of fish from her iron fish dryer and toss it into the palm oil for me. A plate of yam with a naked bowl of palm oil left me feeling less, unworthy. An overwhelming feeling of rejection overcame me. I thought about my father's people, who didn't want us because we had an Igbo mother. I thought about the strange feeling I had for girls, and how that seemed bad. I concluded that maybe I deserved what I got. I was unfit and of no value.

Though I was due to be home at a particular time, the walk home from school was relaxing. That was when I noticed and admired the Nsukka green knolls. The grass was lush and the hills were like giant human guards at sleep. The road down the engineering department looked beautiful with white-painted side slabs. It led all the way to link up Eni Njoku Street, our street. There was something about the silence, being the only one walking down a long, warm road, the chirping birds, the distant cry of solitary hawkers, and passing by houses where I delivered lettuce from my aunt's vegetable garden.

It was at the university primary school I picked up my reading again. It took a while for me to make new friends, but I did find a couple of mates who were willing to lend me books and talk about it with me later. They were mostly books by Enid Blyton and Mills and Boon romance novels. It was there I met two girls who I really liked. One of them was Ihu. I had an intense attraction to her. Intermittently, I visited her, but I didn't realize how strongly I felt about her until we were sprawled on the floor of her living room, just chitchatting. My private parts tingled, and I suddenly leaned over to kiss her.

She gently pushed me off and said, "I am sorry, but I am not a lesbian!"

I wanted to ask her the meaning of the word. Because of the way she seemed alarmed by my attempt to kiss her, I knew the word was not something good. I felt so embarrassed and wished that the earth would open up and swallow me. I got quiet. She got up and brought us some orange juice.

That incident made me begin to think of who and why I liked certain people and not others. When one of the boys in our neighborhood at Nsukka, Victor, started to pay attention to me and secretly lure me behind my uncle's garage to kiss me, and my cousins cheered me on, I wondered if that was the right way to like somebody. At first, I enjoyed the attention but didn't like the way he thrust his tongue into my mouth. But I continued meeting him behind my uncle's garage. My cousins always smiled when they saw us. They didn't call it "lesbian." They didn't disapprove or try to shove me away from him, so that must have been the right thing: kissing a boy and not a girl. Our meetings continued until the day he tried to slide his hand into my underwear. I pushed him away and ran off.

A few days later, when I was playing catch ball with my cousins and one of our neighbors called Zima, I grabbed her to prevent her from catching the ball my cousin threw to her, and a strong sensation, the same one I felt when I met Ihu, overtook me. I clung to her for a while longer and then Ihu's comment rang through my head. I instantly let her go.

She merely giggled and called me a cheat for breaking the rules of the game. "You catch the ball, not the person trying to catch the ball!"

We laughed about it, but thoughts of the sensation bothered me. I wondered if something was wrong with me. Each time I focused on the thought, something sinister hung over me like a dark cloud. Ihu gave it a name and I had to find out what it meant, but I also knew that I had to be careful about who I asked the meaning of the word. Maybe I was possessed. The worry died down as my days picked up with more activities and changes.

10. Tolling Bells

AFTER GRADUATING FROM the University of Nigeria primary school, I was admitted into Urban Girls Secondary School Nsukka. But the notion then was that Queen of the Rosary Secondary School, where most of my mates from the university primary school were enrolled, was a better school, so I transferred to Queen of the Rosary Secondary School also known as Queens Nsukka. It was a Catholic convent boarding school. My uncle had taken the trouble to convey me between both locations to make sure I had a smooth transition to Queens.

It was said to be one of the best girls' schools at that time. It nestled at the foot of huge hills, surrounded by shrubs and a few streams. The quietness that wrapped the school was oftentimes broken by chants of our rosary or the yells from our playground. Between our classes, studies, siesta, meals, and games times were the routine of prayer and labor. But we did manage to wrestle out a life of our own by organizing school parties, conducting dance contests, and indulging in very intense relationships and friendships.

My first night at Queens, I couldn't sleep. I kept roaming around the dormitory like a rat caught in a cage. The next morning, I couldn't take a bath in the school's open bathroom even when I peeked and saw other girls already showering. It was not so much about the crippling Nsukka cold weather as much as it was that I didn't want to expose my body to strangers. I stood there for a while watching them, waiting to see if they would leave early so I could bathe alone. Dawn was already clearing as daylight timidly emerged from the sky. Yet the open bathroom was continually filled.

I was still standing and shivering from the morning winds when a girl, I suppose she was a prefect, asked me why I was there and not entering the bathroom. I didn't say a word, so she hissed and hurried past me. Eventually, the crowd in the bathroom thinned out. There were just a couple of students left. I plucked the courage to remove my clothes while clutching on to my bulky breasts. I did pay the price because I was late for morning prayer and was asked to kneel at the end of the chapel. After morning prayers, we all marched in a straight line and went to our various classes.

My new school reminded me of the classrooms at the university primary school except that the university primary school had more spaces. My first class for the day was French. I didn't realize what class it was until a handsome albino wobbled into the class. He greeted the class with the words "Bonjour! Ça va!" He gestured to us to respond with "Ça va bien!" We did. Then he taught us a song in French. Each time he smiled, his eyes lit up. His love for French was infectious. However, it was my English and literature teacher that got me excited about reading and writing. My mother and grandmother's stories seemed to have followed me to school and to everywhere I went.

My English and literature teacher was pretty. I couldn't tell if her beauty was part of why I was excited about her class. I could gaze at her face all day. Her smooth, soft-looking skin looked like it could peel on a touch. Her smile was captivating, and as if she knew that I was transported to another world with her smile, she flashed it at me with every question I asked. There was also something about her persuasive ways that made me believe I could understand literature more than my classmates. She told me I had a good pair of eyes, that I also had good ears, and was very observant.

Her praise and encouragement motivated me even more to keep learning. I wanted to follow up with her for every assignment she gave us, so I had asked her if I could see her in her office for a task I was finding difficult to grasp. However, she said that I had to ask her in class first before I could come to her office. I didn't want my classmates to know that I wanted to see her at her office after class, so I didn't bother asking her anymore.

My interest in literature continued when one of my most charismatic teachers, Mr. Ogugua, came to teach us the course in my sophomore year of high school. He used his face, limbs, and body language to illustrate every point he made about a character or a theme we were studying. Because of his captivating way of breaking down poetry with figures of speech, I started writing poems. I became so obsessed with writing poems that often when he was teaching, he would insert, "Unoma. Pay attention and stop writing while I am talking."

"Yes, sir!" I'd say.

Apart from writing, and wandering around the school's massive sports field, the only other activity that excited me was our school parties.

One party that left me in awe was the one where a group of girls named Rhythm of the Night Chicks mimed and performed DeBarge's "Rhythm of the Night." As one of the crooners, Ife, belted out the words, her aura absorbed me. Her tall, lean, frame held me bound. The gloss on her lips sparkled as each word soothed me. I had a reason to move my feet, and though self-conscious, I swayed along with her towering presence. I couldn't help but notice her taut, curvy hips. The sound faded, and I was transformed. I felt my timid nerves leap into life. I started singing along, waving my hands in the air as my whole frame shook. All I saw was Ife. The rest of the group members disappeared in the distance. The song hugged my senses as a warm coat would in a cold desert night. I had an instant crush on Ife, but that was a fantasy that had to be quelled. She was a senior, and approaching senior students for even a mere question was suicidal.

One of such experiences I had was with a senior, Ano. I really liked her. I had approached her and asked her if she could be my school mother. She scoffed and asked if I was a fool. Before I could offer an explanation, she hushed me up and asked if I didn't know that she was in a different house than I was. School daughters were only supposed to have school mothers from their own houses to make it convenient for them to serve their school mothers. I must have known that, but for some reason, the fact escaped me. I apologized and said that I didn't know. It didn't end there. I asked her if she could be my mentor. She looked me up and down to my toes and then asked me to kneel next to her bedpost.

"See you, cockroach. You have such guts!"

I kneeled until my knees started burning from the harsh concrete floor. After some hours, I apologized and promised that I would never make stupid requests like that. Then she let me go. However, I didn't stop. Whenever I saw her with her books, I would rush to her and grab them from her to assist her. She would respond with a mixture of disdain and amusement. I was still hopeful. I had held on to the smirk I saw on her face.

One day, when I had followed her with her books to her dormitory, she shocked me. As soon as we stepped inside, she called out to all the seniors in the long and far-reaching hallway with bunk beds stretched out from side to side. "Who will help me deal with this puppy, this little lesbian that keeps following me around like a stray dog?"

My heart pounded against my ribs. I broke out in sweat. I prayed for the floor to open up and swallow me. I made for the door to run out, but she grabbed me. She asked me to kneel. All the seniors surrounded me. She pushed my head. Others kicked my side.

"Look at her dust-caked legs. You are not even worthy to serve anyone of us," a large-faced one said.

Another pushed me and said, "When I am talking to you, how dare you look me in the eye. Are you not afraid? Have you no respect!" She slapped the back of my neck. I kept muttering my apologies.

From a distance, another senior with a cup of what might have been tea strutted toward us. When she reached us, her nose was upturned. "That is how it starts. When they want to hit on you, they request to be your helper, your daughter, your younger sister, your niece, your usher, your whatever! She is not even polished enough to be Ano's chick or girlfriend. That is beside the fact that she is ugly," she yelled and asked me, "You fancied yourself good enough to be Ano's lover?"

"I was only—" I tried to speak.

"Shutttt up, you toad!" she interrupted me and dropped some of her hot tea on my left heel. I winced in pain and tried to get up. "If you move an inch, you will kneel for another two hours. Next time, when you want to hit on a senior prefect, you will think twice. Useless goat!

Before they all dispersed and left me to my shame, I was ordered to scrub their bunk spaces. With all their corners combined and because they were scattered around the long stretch of hall, it was a near-impossible task. I had to scrub and clean their spaces with soap and brush on my knees until the spaces shone like the moon. Even after I cleaned all their spaces, they took turns to inspect and told me to keep scrubbing, that it was not clean enough. They said they would only be satisfied if the floor shone like a plate they could eat from. After that experience, I knew better never to "like" or even "smile" at a senior student.

The day after the incident, I became somewhat withdrawn and ashamed of myself. I formed a routine of walking around our large school field, brooding and reflecting on whether I was sick to find myself often intensely drawn to women. I also wondered why my father left. He left me. I also wondered why my mother didn't visit often.

I continued scribbling verses and what I had called Questions for God. When I thought about my parents, tears flooded my eyes, and I wanted to sit down on the dry grass and cry. But when I looked around, a couple of students were walking toward me. They must have been praying because they were fingering their rosary beads. I didn't want to call attention to myself, so instead of sitting on the grass, I kept walking and wiped my tears with the back of my hand. I brought out the small notepad from my house dress and started scribbling.

Some of the lines I scribbled in the hopes of making it a long poem were: *Loneliness, I feel the loneliness. I am alone, alone in emptiness. Someone, someone is calling. Is that someone me? Daddy.*

Randomly, I added questions: *Why are we here on earth? Why are things difficult? Why do some have, and others do not have? Why would some of my friends always have their parents visit them, but mine hardly do?*

I wished my father was alive or that some of his relatives wanted us. They didn't want us. His death was like a betrayal to me. He could have fought death; I thought he could have. His passing made my spirit recoil. I wanted nothing to do with the world and how it worked. I became even more resolved to hold on to my anger and to rebel in every way I could. Everything I held true left with my father's death. Though my anger wore out, I had less care in the world.

11. Lurching

I COULDN'T THINK ANYMORE. My head was threatening to explode. I couldn't scribble anymore. The evening light was weakening. The bell for evening prayers rang. For prayers, we were in a single line of four rows. We formed a queue behind each other and walked around the east end of the school ground for the fifteen sets of the rosary including the "I Believe" and "Our Father."

The "Hail Mary" chants almost put me to sleep. I was often distracted and found that my eyes settled on the different shapes of my schoolmates' butts. There was a certain beauty to the ways they bounced and swayed in a near musical swing. Each gaze came with a whisper that I'd be forgiven by God. I should be praying, not lusting after women. I exhaled and let the echoes of the prayers soothe my raging nerves.

"Hail Mary, full of grace. The Lord is with you. Blessed are you among women. Blessed is the fruit of thy womb Jesus. Holy Mary, Mother of God, pray for us sinners now and at the hour of our death." We had said our last set of the rosary, as if timed, the bell for dinner rang, and I hurried to my dormitory to get my plate and my school mother's plate.

At the cafeteria, it was somebody else's turn to share out the soup and the fish. In the past, I had argued with whoever was sharing out the fish because they had a way of not being fair with their sharing. I was too tired to let Echi, the girl sharing out the fish and soup, know that I knew she continuously put an extra spoonful of soup in her dish, or yell at her for continuously putting the larger pieces of fish onto her plate. The girl standing next to me, Chiebo, asked if I was okay. We would usually chitchat while waiting for our food. This time, I responded to all her attempts to chat with me with a "hummmmm" or "yes."

As if I was not already having enough bad days, on my way back to my dormitory with my school mother's food I spilled some of the soup. I knew she was going to be upset. I never liked her: Faustina. Even though she ate the food with the remaining soup, she still asked me to kneel beside her bed until my knees hurt. I was whimpering in pain when a short, dark-skinned pretty senior walked up to me and asked me why I was in tears. My school mother was not there, so I narrated the whole incident to her. She rubbed her hands on my head, ruffling my small 'fro, and said, "Awwww, poor cutie. Sorry. You are so cute, too cute to be in tears."

I felt better. I had never had a senior be that nice to me. I picked up the courage and asked her name.

"Yere. What is yours?"

"Unoma."

"It's okay. I will talk to your school mother.

"Thank you," I said. Within a few minutes, my school mother was back. She asked me to get up and go to my bed.

In that same week, I met Yere again and asked her if she would be my school mother. She agreed but maintained that I had to wait for a few more months until my school mother graduated. Faustina did graduate in a few months and Yere became my school mother. She was very protective of me. Inasmuch as I felt loved and cared for, she started censoring the people I became friends with, where I went to, and what I did. Things escalated between us when she wouldn't stop warning me about staying away from Star. I was almost forced to confront her when her constant nagging about Star became unbearable. I was ready to denounce her as a school mother if she continued insisting on coming between us.

When I first met Star and had a crush on her, I was eager to explore my attraction to her. She made me feel comfortable with discovering parts of my body that lit up at her touch. She taught me that it was okay to express my feelings. If I was hesitant about kissing her, she'd cup my cheeks in her hands and kiss me deeply. I learned how to respond and kiss back. She opened me up to love. Though she was a year my senior, it didn't matter to me that she was older.

Because Yere watched us closely, we resorted to hiding at the back of our dormitory at night to kiss. Nothing was going to come between us, not even the school principal. We started a relationship, but I didn't see us as exclusive because I wanted to meet other people and make more friends. She became territorial and possessive, so after a verbal brawl with Yere, she kept away from me, and I gave her some distance with the hope that she would understand she didn't own me.

It was another visiting Sunday a few weeks later. I didn't want to be left alone in the middle of all the excitement of friends and family visits, so I decided to go to the convent: Queen of the Rosary. Except for birds flapping their wings as they perched from tree to tree, there were no other sounds. Occasionally, snorting pigs could be heard from the convent's pigsty. I lingered with my steps, unsure of whether to stand and take in the silence, whisper a prayer and hurry back to my dorm, or try to push forward in search of solace, a place to pray.

At the entrance of the convent, a Caucasian reverend sister smiled into my eyes and introduced herself as Sister Kelly. She was Irish, she said. I looked down at my feet. There seemed to be so much light in her eyes. Maybe it had something to do with the fact that I hadn't been too close to a white person. It felt strange, especially when she reached for my chin and lifted my face.

"Are you okay?" she asked. The light in her eyes faded.

"I want to pray."

"Okay. Let me show you the chapel."

The chapel was wrapped with long, neatly folded white cloth. Slants of light pierced the glass windows behind the chapel table and illuminated the room. As if she read my mind, she pulled the drapes and shut out the sharp sunlight. With her hands clasped as if in prayer, she walked with paced steps. Alone in my thoughts, I was on the verge of tears. I felt like an orphan. I closed my eyes and fought back the tears. I didn't know what to say to God. I didn't know what to think, and I didn't know what to pray about.

I was still trying to gather my scattered feelings together when the bell for our evening prayers rang. It was okay to pray with the sisters, though they prayed like us, the students, by standing in a row of three or four as they recited the rosary and walked along the long path that led to the exit and entry gate of the convent. We had the same prayer schedule sometimes. I heard some sisters scamper out of their halls and outside.

A couple came into the chapel, glanced at me and sat behind me. The other genuflected before the Blessed Sacrament and then sat in front of me but to the far left. We were submerged in silence. After a few more minutes, when I heard other sisters coming back. I got up, bowed before the Blessed Sacrament and stepped out of the chapel. On my way out, I saw Sister Kelly. It felt as if she was waiting for me.

"You want to drink something? Water? Juice?" Her warm and welcoming presence made me happy. Their guest and waiting room was scantily decorated. There were a couple of side tables and a rose-littered curtain on two long windows of the room. There was also a bookshelf, and I was tempted to look through the books. There were mostly religious books and a few novels by Bronte and George Eliot. My eyes were still on the bookshelf when Sister Kelly returned.

"You like reading?" she asked me as she placed the tray containing a box of orange juice, water, and cookies on one of the small side table. She pulled the table close to me and asked if she could pour either water or orange juice. I asked for the orange juice.

"Yes. I like reading. My mother read to me as a child."

"Really? That is good. What books have you read that you like?" she asked with her hands akimbo. I could feel the excitement in her voice. It seemed infectious.

"I see Bronte on your shelf here. I loved reading *Jane Eyre*. But I was shaken by finding myself hauled into the attic with the deranged lady."

"Interesting," she said with a scowl. "Any others?"

"Yes. I have read all the series of Famous Five and Secret Seven."

"Who wrote those?"

"Enid Blyton. I really love George in Famous Five," I said, almost choking as I downed the whole glass of orange juice.

"Easy. Are you okay?"

"Yes," I said, clearing my throat.

"So why do you like George? Was he a good character?"

"She! She reminds me of me."

"How?"

"She stands up to boys and does not take any nonsense."

"I see! And you do not take any nonsense?" she asked with a chuckle.

"No," I said between bites of cookie.

"At least there are no boys to worry about here."

"But there are some girls here that are worse than boys," I said, sipping my juice this time.

"I wouldn't be surprised. But that is why we need to pray often and read our bibles to know how to deal with people and find out ways to forgive them when they offend us. Start coming for bible studies."

I promised her that I would come whenever I was not attending the one in school. I also wanted to come back to spend more time with her and to see more of the light in her eyes when she smiled.

I was back on time for our night meal at the cafeteria. I was not too eager to eat the pebble-infested beans we were normally served since I had filled up with the cookies and juice Sister Kelly gave me, but I had to get my school mother's meal. When I dropped her food in her bunk bed space, one of my former bunkmates, Nwaka, invited me for what she called a night vigil. I was not too keen on vigils and noisy prayers, but she promised me that there would be movies there too. Eagerly, I followed her to the vigil. That sounded better than lying on my bunk bed brooding about my life and being sad about not having my parents the way my other schoolmates had their parents visiting them all the time.

When we got there, the place was rowdy with squeals from praying students. I wanted to walk out, but Nwaka tugged at my hand and said the movies came later. The prayers finally ended, and the pastor started preaching. He preached about weaknesses and how we shouldn't let our flaws and weaknesses control us. He gave the example of Samson. I couldn't tell why, but all of a sudden, my heart started thumping. I knew my weakness. I knew my sin. Maybe I needed to talk to somebody about it. But I hadn't really done anything wrong.

Within an hour, the pastor made an altar call for those who wanted to get rid of their sins and weaknesses. People started walking toward him. He stood at the middle of the altar and those who walked out surrounded the podium where he stood. He started praying for them. Then he jumped down from the podium and rushed into the crowd. "There is somebody here who likes girls, the way a boy should love a girl. She has a weakness for women. She is possessed."

That was very strange. My head was down as my heart threatened to jump out of my chest. Under my breath, I cussed Nwaka. When he seemed to have gone a bit farther away from where I was standing, I looked at the door to see if it was open. As if he saw me, he made for my direction. He stood beside me, sweaty and panting as he screeched, "Water spirits shall not possess you. These demons that serve the goddess of the deep seas, Mammy Water, will be removed from you! That Mammy Water and all her servant spirits do not want you to have a husband. She has sealed your fate with your lust for women because she has maintained you as a wife in the marine underworld. That evil spirit of lesbianism must get out of you. I shall break that chain of bondage she has placed on you!"

He dragged me by the neck to the center of the podium where everybody else was. Still focused on me, he pushed and shoved me as he continued yelling at Mammy Water and her water agents to set me free in Jesus' name. I knew the routine. I played along. But, besides feeling like a spectacle and embarrassed, it was the force of his hands that hurt me the most. He pushed me until I fell and he leaned over me, with saliva bursting out of his mouth and landing on my face. I tried to protect myself with my hands, but he untwisted them.

As he stamped his feet next to my head, he was still pressing me down on the floor. For a second, I thought he would either stamp me to death or strangle me. How was he able to pin me down and stamp his right foot at the same time? Fear gripped me. I leaped up and made for the door, but he asked his aides to grab me. They did. It was futile for me to keep resisting. That made him more hostile and aggressive. I could feel the burn in my elbow from my peeled skin. My neck and ears were throbbing from the pressure he'd applied when he'd held me down.

When his aides brought me to him, he started spinning me as he shouted, "Get away from her. Get away from her!"

I kept spinning until I lost balance and fell. He kneeled beside me and wouldn't relent. I just decided to lie still. I tried to look out at the crowd. Most of them were praying, but I could have sworn I caught a glimpse of Nwaka's snickering face. I closed my eyes and felt goose bumps all over my body.

The pastor came at me again and asked, "Do you accept Jesus as your personal Christ and Savior?"

"I do!"

"Do you agree to cut all ties with the sins of the flesh and to surrender your life to Christ?

"I do!"

"Good," he said and helped me up before he walked away to gather the rest of the people who were standing and praying. He told us all to stand close to him as we gathered together in the middle, and he asked the choir to sing to welcome new lambs to the fold of God. I was relieved. I was no longer the focus of the service. I kept looking at the doors to see if I could leave at some point, but three to four ushers were rooted there. I hoped it meant the pastor was about to wrap up, but that was not the case. They were setting up to show a movie. That must have been the movie Nwaka had mentioned. The thought of that being the only truth to the impression she gave me about the vigil dominated my mind for a while, and I looked around to find her, but she was nowhere in sight. I was convinced she'd told the pastor something strange about me. His focus on me seemed as if he knew me before. That was something I had to settle with Nwaka.

As the movie projector was set up, we were asked to go back to our seats. Even though I had looked forward to seeing a movie, it was not what I expected. The movie showed the wailings of sinners who ended up in hell. I broke out in sweat. I didn't want to go to hell. This time, I willingly stepped out to give my life to Christ. The pastor prayed over me and some other students who had stepped out. Some of them were familiar faces, and I wondered what type of sin they were repenting from—if any of them had my kind of sin.

I left the vigil angry and remorseful. I was angry at Nwaka and sorry about my sin. I didn't know if I should go after the lying, wicked Nwaka or go to my dormitory and cry. I decided to go to my dorm. I didn't cry. I prayed for forgiveness. That didn't stop the thought of Star from floating through my mind. I longed for her. But each time I thought of her, I made the sign of the cross.

12. Sahel

T HE NEXT VISITING Sunday as usual, I didn't have any visitors.
My mother lived far away. My uncle in town was too busy.
So I resorted to staring at visiting parents and their kids with
admiration. I would often swallow lumps of saliva as their parents
scooped out the pieces of meat and fish from the food bowls they
brought with them. As the only way to get to a spoonful of rice
or a piece of meat, I would offer to wash and get more plates for
them. I got useful enough to earn a plate of rice topped with a
bottle of Coke or Fanta, and that would make my Sunday before
I left the dormitory to take a long walk and reflect on my life and
why my fate turned out the way it did. The dry air that clung to
my ashy skin had a way of emphasizing the dry spell on my mind.

Clusters of floating plastic bags and papers stretched through
open fields and spaces as a solitary chicken scratched the earth
for food. It was a rare sight to see because chickens were almost
extinct. Students would usually chase after them, kill them, and
make a sumptuous meal out of them. That day was filled with
food and amusement. Nobody was ever full enough to see a
live chicken scratching and clucking for food. Even though the
chicken was moving freely and going about its business, I felt
sorry for it just as I felt sorry for myself. I never had anyone visit
me. I seemed to be in trouble for liking people. I didn't know why
my father died early. I didn't know why Nwaka would lie to me
and plot to have me delivered from my sin and humiliated. I had
tried to find her, but it was obvious that she had been avoiding me

since the vigil incident. But I planned to go back to the convent. Sister Kelly seemed to like me. I could talk to her.

I got to a bend, at the edge of our cafeteria and the farthest dormitory from mine, house five, when I bumped into another student. It was her bow legs I noticed first and then her smile and thick lips. She had a stunning smile too. I was surprised because most students were either with their visitors or at the dorm eating their friends' or neighbors' food, especially if they had no visitors. I was not sure about asking her why she didn't have a visitor or where she was coming from.

"Hey!" she eventually said to me. We had lingered a bit with our smiles and stares.

"Hey!" I said. "What is your name? What are you doing here? You don't have visitors?"

"Not this time. I am Uzo. My parents were here not too long ago. I went to the canteen to get snacks, but the canteen man isn't there," she said, tugging at the white, twisted belt around her waist.

"Oh! He is usually there at this time," I responded and grabbed her belt with a hard pull. She laughed, and I laughed too. I was just being playful even as I hoped she would not be offended. She was so warm. It felt as if we had known each other for a long time.

"No visitors for you either?"

"I hardly ever have visitors. What is your dorm?"

"House six."

"House six? How come I have never seen you before?"

"I don't know. How come I have never seen you before?"

We both laughed again and decided to walk to her dorm together. As we walked, we talked. I found her husky voice intriguing. She also seemed intelligent and funny.

When we got to her dorm and her bunk bed, she made some tea and offered me some with a Cabin biscuit. I turned it down and watched her eat. She kept looking at me and giggling.

I giggled back. We asked each other more questions about school, our families, and about life. Her parents were engineers, and they lived in Lagos with her two younger brothers. She lay down, and mischief came over me. I balanced my frame over her. We kept talking. It was the red hue of the low sun that made me realize that we had been talking for hours. It streamed in through the high glass window and hung like a light, rosy curtain draped across her bunk bed.

"Tell me about your life plans," she said with half-shut, dreamy eyes. I wouldn't have noticed how long her lashes were if she didn't keep darting them as if struggling to keep her eyes open.

"That is a deep question. You are getting too serious for me." We laughed.

"You look like somebody I have seen before. Are you in the drama and debating society?"

"Yes. How do you know?"

"That's it! I watched you speak when our school had a debating competition with Isienu Boys. I thought you were stern and cute."

"Thanks, but am I not still cute?"

"You are." We both laughed again.

I looked away from her and focused on her glowing, dark-chocolate skin. There was a long stretch of thin scar across the hollow of her right arm. I tracked it with the tip of my index finger, wondering how she got it. Then out of the blue, she gently pulled me to her lips and kissed me, but I pulled away when somebody rushed through her dorm door and slammed it violently. It was scrawny Ebe. She hurried to Uzo's corner. Out of breath, she glared at me.

"What are you doing here?" she demanded.

"What do you mean? Are we in the wrong corner?" I asked, looking at Uzo for confirmation. She waved at me not to say another word.

"Ebe, I didn't realize I needed your permission to either make new friends or have a guest."

"At least you should have mentioned that you were expecting Unoma Azuah."

Uzo sighed and didn't say any more. I thought that was enough sign for Ebe to leave, but no. She sat opposite me, on Uzo's neighbor's bunk bed, and kept glaring at me.

I'd met Ebe at the drama society I had auditioned for. We were both accepted but she had insisted on taking the role the group offered me. Because of her, we had to audition twice and I won. After that, she was always hostile and aggressive toward me. There was no way I would have known or guessed that Uzo was her "chick" as we called our "special" friends then. And even if I'd known, I wouldn't have cared enough to worry about whether she would approve of my friendship with Uzo or not.

Her presence at Uzo's corner felt like another contest. She didn't move an inch. I stayed with Uzo until darkness crept in through the glass windows. More students thronged into the dorm. It was not until I saw Nwaka walk in with her fat bible that I leaped up and chased after her. Uzo wondered where I was headed to as she screamed out my name. Her voice faded in the background as I grabbed Nwaka's collar and pulled her toward me.

"Stupid girl! I yelled. "Was that your uncle you deceived me into attending his vigil? I shoved her around, trying to force the truth out of her mouth.

"Leave me alone! The devil has come over you again. I thought the pastor cast it away."

I pushed her to the ground and was about to pounce on her to deal her some blows when Uzo pulled me away.

"You know you will be suspended if you fight, Unoma!"

I backed away with my fist still clenched.

"I have no business with you except to preach the gospel to you and your kind, who lust after women like you," Nwaka said as she adjusted her collar and picked up her bible.

Uzo led me back to her corner, and Ebe, who had been encouraging Nwaka to fight back, came and sat down on her spot. We all sat in silence until the bell for prayers rang. Uzo took her scarf and her rosary from under her pillow and asked that we go for prayers together. Ebe still sat there like a fool. I inched closer to her and said, "Bye-bye, bitch." She rolled her eyes at me. I was hoping that she would as much as touch me, but Uzo pulled me away. After prayers, we hugged and promised to see each other again.

Eagerly, I went to Uzo's corner the next day. I was taken aback when she said she didn't want to speak to me. Star had been to see her the night before and threatened to beat her up if she didn't stay away from me—which was shocking, because after the snake incident and a display of her jealousy, we had given each other some space. I figured she'd got the message. Apparently not, otherwise she would not be warning Uzo to stay away from me. Then Ebe came to mind, and the only urge I had was to find her, beat her, and willingly offer myself up to be suspended from school.

On a second thought, I decided to take a break from all three of them and preoccupied myself with writing poetry and watching any social events that would distract me and keep me entertained. Our house parties offered such opportunities. I would only watch and admire. I didn't think I was much of a dancer until I watched the Rhythm of the Night Chicks. If there was anything the Rhythm of the Night Chicks gave me, it was the inspiration to mime and perform a song or at least act as a disc jockey.

For one of the parties, I acted as a DJ and also mimed a song. I had to borrow shiny clothes to appear like a true DJ. I combed and oiled my hair, which I rarely did because I had little patience for the extra demand looking good required. I wrote and rehearsed my DJ lines several times. I was nervous. I didn't want to mess up and embarrass myself, especially in the presence of some of the girls I admired. So, before the day, I had become comfortable with phrases like:

"You are all welcome to the party ground and we are going to rock the house till the break of dawn."

"Don't get too nasty with those dance moves."

"Dance with somebody. Feel the heat with somebody."

I thought I stumbled over each word, but my performance impressed my mates. I was happy, though. I became familiar with most of the lyrics I used from a habit of listening to my cousin's songs. Being a DJ was not a regular thing, but I enjoyed the attention it got me while it lasted. Feeding off the popularity I garnered overnight, I became the school clown. I got so good at clowning and cracking jokes that my friends dubbed me "Wodu Wakiri"—the village entertainer from Elechi Amadi's novel, *The Concubine*.

The crowd of people I had as friends complicated some of my relationships with them. Some became possessive, jealous, and wanted my company for almost all of the day. Some felt threatened by the appearance of new friends. The tension this situation brought led to a fight between some of my friends. I got called everything from "Player!" and "Slut" to "Clown." At first, it felt good to be popular and to be wanted, but I worried about being invited to the principal's office for lashes. I would break up fights depending on who caught me in a compromising position and announce that I wanted nothing to do with any of them. That strategy worked. I decided to keep few friends and wondered why we all just couldn't be one happy family. But in spite of the popularity I enjoyed, I still felt very lonely. Then I met Nelo.

13. A Sky of Stars

I WAS CLOSE TO some of my teachers, especially the French teacher, Monsieur, and my literature teacher, Mr. Ogugua. Monsieur would invite me to his office and try to teach me French by talking to me only in French. I tried to respond in French as best as I could, but we ended up laughing at each other. He told me about French writers and French literature. I liked him and he was kind to me. Often, he brought me food and snacks when he came to school. I never told my friends and my bunk neighbors where I got the snacks and food from. It was supposed to be our little secret, Monsieur's and mine. He was intelligent and had a great sense of humor, and I looked up to him and enjoyed spending time with him—until he invited me to his house on a weekend visit.

He told me he could help me get permission to go home for a day. He did. He asked me to come alone. With the directions he gave me, I was to meet him at a junction under a huge Udala tree, just before a local market. I got there and he was waiting.

At his house, he had already cooked a delicious pot of stew and rice. We ate, chatted, told jokes, and laughed. We sat on his cozy couch. I was reading a magazine I picked up from his table. He sat next to me and held me. I wriggled out of his grip. He still got closer. I sat up from the chair, and he playfully wobbled his way to me. He had a bad leg. As he walked, the bad leg wasn't quite strong enough to steady him, so he wobbled with every step. When I refused to sit down, he promised to stop bothering

79

me. I sat, and he flopped next to me and tried to kiss me. All I could feel were dry, prickly lips with his warm breath that stank of fish. I pulled away, and he apologized.

Though I left his house with bread, sugar, and some cans of milk, I vowed never to return. That didn't stop him. At one point, he proposed to me. I was honest and confident enough to tell him that I liked him, but I didn't find him attractive. He laughed it off and told me it was a phase.

"Girl crushes often happen in all-girls schools. It will pass. Think about my proposal," he said to me with his unsteady eyes. Because he was an albino, his pupils were always darting around even when he squinted them under the sharp lights of intense sun rays. I started avoiding him. I started resenting him for dismissing my feelings. He didn't even want to discuss it or even ask me if I had a girlfriend or somebody I really liked. Instead, he rendered my feelings irrelevant. How dare he? But, I wondered, what was I thinking? I should have known that preying on girls was mostly seen as normal. It was an acceptable culture. If anything had happened and I'd complained, I would have been blamed for going to his house in the first place.

Though I never discussed my love for girls with Mr. Ogugua, he was more accepting of me, especially when he read the poems I dedicated to girls in school. He would call my poems beautiful and not ask me personal questions. He would often talk about my use of metaphors and alliteration and suggest some ways I could improve on the poems. He didn't question who I expressed my love for and how.

Because Mr. Ogugua was often looking out for what I was doing in class when he suspected that I was not paying attention, I changed my tactic. I waited to write when he turned to write on the board. One day, I was not writing poetry. I had written a quick note to Nelo, a pretty girl I noticed for the first time in my class. Her narrow eyes and oval face were unique. I liked her instantly. Then I snuck the note under my desk and lightly touched her leg with it.

At first, she frowned because she was in the middle of taking down the teacher's notes. I had written: "I like you, but I am not a lesbian." She read it and giggled at me. That was not the reaction I was expecting, but it felt good. I proceeded to draft a poem for her. That was when I got carried away and forgot all about Mr. Ogugua. He caught me and asked me to show him what I was writing. I walked up to him as the whole class stared. I held my breath, hoping he wouldn't ask me to read it out loud. He glanced at it.

"You are writing a poem?"

"Yes."

"Not during class. See me after class."

"Yes, sir," I said, relieved.

For my punishment, he asked me to write a poem a day using all the figures of speech he taught in class. I was to show him the poems once every week.

When I was done talking to Mr. Ogugua, I was glad to discover that Nelo was at a corner waiting for me with the note. Her penetrating eyes made me look away. She was the sun.

"What is a lesbian?" she asked loudly though still smiling.

"Ssshhhh!" I whispered and looked around to make sure nobody heard her.

She frowned and her smile disappeared. "Why? Is it something bad?"

"I don't know, but I think so."

"So how do you know about the word?"

"A friend used it."

"I have an idea. Let's look it up in the dictionary."

"Sure," I said, even though I'd looked up the word after Ihu mentioned it.

We were on our way back to our classroom locker to retrieve her dictionary when we ran into a prefect. She asked if we were freshmen, told us that we were supposed to get our plates from our dormitories and head to the refectory. I asked Nelo what dormitory she was and if she had a school mother. She told me that she was in House 7 and that she had a school mother. We agreed to meet in the refectory. After lunch, I followed her to her dorm to know where her space was located. House 7 was closer to the refectory. Her bunk was close to the end of the bed-filled open hall, just a couple of beds away from the end wall. I noted her bed and turned to leave. She gave me a rushed hug and made me promise that I would come back. My heart was glad and fluttered with tentative excitement.

After the meal, we had a few minutes' interval before our afternoon nap. I gave my school mother her food; she hadn't quite taken the plates when she yelled at me for not putting our plastic containers in the queue for water. She warned me to make sure she had water to bathe in the morning and that she didn't care how or where I got it from. With two large plastic containers, I rushed out to the queue. I got hopeful when I observed that the water queue was steadily getting shorter.

What I dreaded about not having my water containers out early was that when that happened, I was likely to be caught by senior prefects on rounds to get those who were not obeying the afternoon nap rule. I was able to fill my containers and lugged them together, one in each hand. It was a struggle, but I did it. If I had tried to carry one in and then come back for the other, somebody could have stolen it.

In spite of the strain of school chores, the thought of Nelo warmed my heart. I looked forward to seeing her during our study hours. When time for evening studies came, I ran up to my class, eager to see Nelo again. After thirty minutes when there were no signs of her, my eyes kept darting toward the windows hoping she'd appear.

An hour went by, and there was no Nelo. I grabbed my books and went searching for her. I didn't know where to look, but for some reason, I kept looking under trees with chairs. She was nowhere. I had to be careful not to run into prefects who were patrolling to make sure everyone was in their study room. I ran into one who waved her long whip at me and then asked me why I was not in my study room. I explained that I needed to use the toilet. She let me go. I circled the block of our classroom and saw Nelo under a tree stringing through her rosary and muttering the Hail Mary. I sat next to her. She held my hand and squeezed it. Her dashing smile brightened up her face. Then she dug her hand into the pocket of her blue uniform and pulled out another rosary. She tossed it at me.

"Why are you here saying the rosary when in the next hour or so we will be doing exactly the same thing?"

"Extra prayers don't hurt. How did you find me?"

"I looked."

"What do you mean by you looked?"

"I was hoping you would come to the study room. When I didn't see you, I decided to look. Something told me to look under the shaded trees."

"Why? Do I look like a squirrel?" She laughed.

"No. I just had the feeling I should look there."

"I wanted you to come and look for me."

"Okay. What if prefects see us here?"

She pulled me, grabbed my hand, and led me to a hidden spot with low shrubs. There were a couple of trees with birds' nests. It was cozy and felt safe from the senior prefects' prying eyes. But I was still uncomfortable with the idea of being caught there.

"Nobody will see us, I promise," she said with that her dashing smile again. "Let's say the rosary for a few minutes."

"The rosary? That would take all day!"

"Just a few Our Fathers and a few Hail Marys will do. We don't have to say it together," she said and playfully pinched my cheeks.

She was about my age, but there was something so mature and in control about her and the way she expressed herself. That was also one of the things I found attractive about her. She took charge and was almost self-assured about everything.

I couldn't focus on my Hail Marys. I couldn't help but stare at her cleavage and the long angle of her neck and nape. I soaked in her presence the way I would take in a soothing stream or the comforting crash of a waterfall.

She looked at me, grabbed my hand again and squeezed it. "Focus. Say your prayers," she said.

I needed the prayers, any prayers that would save me from the tumultuous wallops of my heart. My whole body responded to her, and it was scary; something I couldn't explain. My attraction to her was intense. She was so beautiful and I couldn't believe that my fantasy of her wanting me as much as I wanted her was possible. I wanted to take her and put her inside of me: safe and secure. Out of impulse, I lay on her thigh, and it felt like cushions of clouds, cradling and warm. Warmth seemed to rise from her and seep into my cold chest and my whole body. This felt like home. This was where I belonged.

All the comfort and peace I sought, I seemed to have found here, on her thigh. I closed my eyes, but the chatter of two birds remained persistent. I opened my eyes again and watched them preen before darting between the tree branches. I had managed to whisper a number of Hail Marys when the voices of the nuns next to our school fence floated over. Their voices drowned out the chatter of the chirping birds, though the nuns' song intermittently encroached and receded. The wind swayed the song back and forth in waves of hums and murmur. All the while, Nelo looked into the distance whispering her prayers. The hymn was familiar. I often listened to my mother when she sang it. There was something nostalgic and mournful about "Sinful Sighing to be Blest." In my head, every word was echoing in my mother's voice, especially as the nuns got to the fourth verse:

From this sinful heart of mine
To Thy bosom I would flee
I am not my own but Thine:
God be merciful to me.

Each word resonated with my feelings for Nelo. Perhaps my feelings for her were sinful, but to her bosom I had fled. I was no longer me but hers. Maybe God would be merciful to me. I looked at her, and she smiled down at me and whispered her last Our Father before she ruffled my hair and said that it was time to leave. We stuck out our heads from our hiding place, using the leaves as camouflage to make sure there were no wandering prefects. We looked in all directions before scampering out and ducked into our classrooms.

After our study period, we went to her dormitory together. Her bed was secured with a long piece of wrapper that she tied around the hinges; there was no bunkmate above her.

"Why do you tie a wrapper around your bed?" I asked.

"I do that to keep the sun away. It blinds my eyes whenever I want to take a siesta."

"Your house prefect allows you to do that?"

"Yes. I asked for her permission."

"I see."

"Sit down. What can I entertain you with? Some Cabin biscuits? I can make some tea to go with them if you are hungry."

Before I could respond, the bell for the cafeteria rang. For some reason, I felt angry. There were always disruptions. There were always bells ringing for one thing or the other. This place felt like a prison. I said a quick goodbye with a hurried hug, then ran to my dormitory to get my school mother's plates for dinner. All my excitement was short-lived. I hoped we were having rice and stew for dinner.

In the refectory, food was divided among the tables. There were five to six students per table, and each table had a pot of garri and soup. Sometimes the soup was too watery, or the rice and beans had small pebbles. I had the responsibility of dividing up the food. Nobody appointed me, but I volunteered as often as I wanted. Occasionally, students accused me of not doing a good job. At one point, one of the girls at the table, Amaka, who had a large head, yelled at me, "Unoma, the fish on your plate is bigger than others."

"Bigger how?" I said. "I shared the fish equally."

"No, yours is bigger!" she yelled.

I shoved my plate to her and snatched hers, but she pulled it back, spilling some of the Ogbono soup. I clenched my fist and glared at her. I didn't want to get into trouble by fighting. Otherwise, I would have punched her big head. The rest of the girls at the table told me to calm down and to ignore her.

I got food for my school mother and brought it back to our dormitory, House 5. There was still a long line of containers in front of the water tank, and that annoyed me. My containers had been in the line for hours. I was tired and ready for the afternoon rest, but there were about fifteen containers ahead of mine. As I waited, I saw Echi sneak up to the water tank and look around to see if anyone was watching her. I looked down so she wouldn't notice that I had seen her. Then she pushed her blue container next to the second one in line.

"What do you think you're doing?" I cried.

Echi rolled her eyes at me. "Unoma Azuah, mind your business!"

"Take that container to the back of the line," I said, pointing at the trail of containers.

She hissed and started to walk away, leaving her container where it was. I kicked it out of the queue. She picked it up and left.

A few minutes later, the line moved, and I pushed my container forward, glad to be moving ahead.

14. Whips

UNOMA AZUAH! UNOMA Azuah, your name is on the list!"
I didn't recognize the voice calling out my name. She had to be one of the new prefects. My heart pounded. A couple of weeks before, two girls had fought in House 4. When they were asked why they fought, they said it was because of me. Even though I didn't ask them to fight over me, I was still told to cut the overgrown grass near the staff quarters.

I whispered a prayer and asked, "What list? Why is my name on the list?"

"You have a lover. You people have sex. You do *supe*. Other girls are kneeling down in front of the principal's office. Go and join them."

There were about a dozen of us kneeling. The jagged stones ground into my knees and pierced my nerves. The sun's heat bore down with heavy hands. It was not long before the principal's whip snapped upon my back. I squealed in pain and begged for forgiveness. Instead, the principal punctuated every lash by saying, "Remember this pain when you commit your sinful act!"

After giving us all uncountable lashes, the principal strutted into her office in a huff. We were to kneel under the intense heat for another hour. When we were finally dismissed, I could still feel the pain breathing through the slashed surface of my back. I didn't want to feel the judgmental gaze of my bunkmates, so I climbed the stairs to my classroom and cried. I was not in there for long before one of the "Born Again" girls came in with a bible.

"Unoma, God loves the sinner but not the sin. I came to pray for you."

"I don't need your prayers," I said.

"You're not ready to renounce your sin?"

"Leave me alone!"

"The spirit of lesbianism is stubborn and demonic. I can start prayers and deliverance for you now, if you believe."

I looked at Ngozi as she talked about prayer and deliverance. Our eyes met. A chill crept down my spine. There was fire in her eyes, with sparks of madness. I moved away from her. I sat by the open window and gazed out. A couple of yellow birds chirruped and darted around the hibiscus flowers scattered around our classroom building. Their chirps drowned out the echoes of Ngozi's prayers as she slammed the bible hard against her lap, casting out demons. That's when I heard them again, the hymns of the reverend sisters coming from the convent next to our school. Their hymns were constant. The song was soothing but mournful at the same time. It settled like a blanket of melancholy over my shoulders. That could be my place of refuge: the convent.

I sat in the empty classroom and fought the urge to cry again. I didn't care if any prefect met me there and punished me for not being where I was supposed to be at that time. Light started giving way to night as darkness gradually enveloped me. The sounds of a lone bird seemed to compete with screeching crickets. A single streetlight pierced through the dark, and a cluster of flying insects incessantly cycled it. I thought I heard Nelo's voice and sat up. It felt as if I suddenly realized I was alone and got scared. I heard my name again. It was between a whisper and a yell. I recognized the voice. It *was* Nelo.

"I am here, Nelo!"

She hurried to me and hugged me, but I winced because she had squeezed my aching back.

"I am sorry. I have turned the whole school upside down looking for you. You shouldn't be here alone in the dark. Let's go to my dorm and I can put Vaseline on your wounds."

For the first time, an intense urge to run away overwhelmed me. Not even my love and attention to Nelo could stop me. We were not allowed to leave the school premises without permission, and to get permission, we had to apply for the permit way in advance. I was often tempted to walk out of our school gate on a Friday when hawkers were allowed to come to our school fence to sell their snacks. Mr. Okoro, the tobacco-stained, two-toothed gateman, would often belligerently warn us not to run wild like bush fowls since we'd been set free for some hours.

Outside that school gate, my eyes often followed the long trail of the windy Ede-Oballa road as it snaked its way downhill to Nsukka town. But following the path beside the road would make it easy for people to see me. Milipat Hotel, right at the top of the hill next to the road, presented a hidden option to escape, but walking up to Milipat seemed even more dangerous because I could be accused of meeting men there to frolic all night long. There had been cases of girls who were said to have gone there and come back pregnant. Such stories were difficult for me to believe until I ran into a crowd of girls in commotion. They had gathered around what was said to be a human fetus.

Nelo was so caring and concerned about the wounds on my back. She gave me her wrapper to tie and asked me to lie on her bed. As she applied the Vaseline, it burned, and I moaned and winced. But the sudden jerk of the cloth she tied around her bunk bed made me shut my mouth.

"What are you people doing?" some random girl asked with a squeaky voice and a smirk.

"What does it look like we are doing, stupid?" Nelo hushed her away and muttered something about how people do not mind their business. I smiled at her firmness but knew to shut my mouth when she applied the Vaseline. I didn't want us to be misunderstood, which might warrant more cane strokes.

My punishment for being accused of lusting after girls didn't end with the strokes of the cane. I also had to clean out the bathroom in my dormitory. The stench and pile of caked feces and bloodied pads violently invaded all my senses. I had to run out to puke. I was bent over, trying to vomit all the smell that had oozed into my nose and mouth. When I steadied myself, I stood firm to take a deep breath. I thought about how to approach the task ahead of me. With one hand over my nose, I gathered all the pads and dry shit into a pile, but the clustered mass of maggots I encountered was unexpected. I splashed a huge amount of water on the floor with the hope that the maggots and most of the dry shit would be moistened and float out to the courtyard. But they just gathered and floated in a stagnant pool. I got a long broom and gently swept them through the tunnels that emptied behind the bushes of our dormitory. With a fairly clean floor, I was able to walk around, still trying to figure out how to flush the stuffed toilets and wash them.

I had incessantly washed the third toilet when I realized that it was stuffed with pads. So I had to poke out all the pads. Each jab forced water to fly at my face. I decided to leave that toilet and go to the next. The sight of an overflowing mound of red, spongy fire ants made me squeal, and I steadied myself and scampered out to the courtyard to take a breath. A bunch of girls were at the shaded end of the courtyard, chattering about washing their school uniforms. I felt like smacking them across their faces for not even being curious enough to ask me why I howled. I tiptoed back to the toilet to peek at the ants.

They were still there. The creepy sight of all those fire ants would have been a relief to behold if I were on my period. My menstrual cramps always felt like vicious fire ants were eating away at my uterus. Looking at them—the embodiment of what

I felt—somehow eased the pain. I invested hours watching clusters of fire ants. However, that day was not the day. I didn't know what to do because scattering them with my stick would have been a disaster. I decided to boil some water in a bucket.

Determined to kill all of them, I splashed the bucket of water on them and gleefully watched them wriggle to their deaths. I swept their splattered bodies through the same tunnels to the bushes behind. I hadn't got to the fourth toilet when the menacing sight of wriggling maggots assailed my eyes. I sighed and dropped the bucket and sticks I had. There was no way I could deal with this. A quick idea hovered around my head. I shook it away, but it wouldn't let me be. I walked to the courtyard and waited. When a crowd of girls gathered at the courtyard to play cards and Ludo, I decided to pass out. I heard screams.

"Unoma Azuah has fainted, Oh! Somebody bring water! Go and tell the matron!"

I tried hard not to smile. The splash of water on my face increased my heartbeat, but I didn't move an inch. The matron came almost immediately and asked a couple of girls to take me to the sick bay. While there, the matron scattered more water on my face and asked me if I could hear her. She kept pressing down her thumb on my wrist, I guess to take my pulse.

Within a couple of hours, my uncle arrived. He took me straight to the University of Nigeria, Nsukka hospital. Dr. Ndukwe attended to me immediately. He took my vitals and asked me if I needed a break from school. There was a conniving smirk on his face. I was not sure what to say to him. I just kept a straight face. I was given a couple of bags of drips and put on bed rest for a couple of days. However, when my uncle came to check on me, I was surprised when the doctor told him that I was all right; all I needed was crayfish.

After forty-eight hours in the hospital, I got tired of being there and decided to walk home. I made for the toilet and snuck out through the back door. The terrain was familiar to me because it was not far from the church I frequented with my aunt and cousins: St Peter's Cathedral. On its far left was my former elementary school. I walked past Balewa Hall and hunkered through Mary Slessor Hall to negotiate my way through the Agriculture Department, and then through the long, winding, dusty road that led straight to the Kemes' house and, next to them, my uncle's house. As soon as I stepped into the compound, my aunt's blaring Congolese Makossa music welcomed me.

My aunt was at her sewing machine, stamping away. I didn't want to startle her, so I called out, "Good evening, Ma!"

She was surprised to see me. "You are not supposed to be at the hospital?"

I told her I'd gotten tired and decided to come home. She insisted that I was supposed to wait for the doctor to discharge me. I was quiet until she asked if I had had a meal. She served me some jollof rice.

The next morning, my uncle took me back to school. It was a Sunday. I paid Sister Kelly a visit. She hugged me with an extra squeeze, and her vanilla fragrance lingered on my nose. When she told me she had looked for me and was told I had fainted, and that she got worried, my smile became a wide grin. She didn't know how to reach me, she said.

In their guest room, we sat down, and she asked why I fainted and if I was okay. I managed to convince her that I was fine, and she offered me fruit juice and cookies, like the last time. Then she asked if I prayed often and went for my confession and masses. When I responded in the affirmative, she informed me of a bible session Sister Charity was conducting. She made me promise I would attend. I did. I had to leave because she needed to run some errands in town. The goodbye hug didn't linger. I was a bit disappointed because I was really drawn to her, but it was not like the way I felt for Nelo. Maybe I looked at her like a mother. I knew

I had no business having a crush on a reverend sister. That would be a bad sin. But she held my hand until we reached the door.

Bible study was boring as usual, but I tried to pay attention, and I even took notes. The stories shared during our bible and moral instructions were not always from the bible. The sisters often focused on the lives of saints like Saint Fatima and Maria Goretti. She was crowned a martyr because she chose to die rather than lose her purity. We admired Maria Goretti, and her moral became an ideal a lot of us chose to live by. Some said they preferred to live pure lives and therefore didn't encourage any relationship with the opposite sex. They kept no boyfriend, and no boy that was not their relatives visited them. It didn't make any difference to me who did or didn't visit me. It even made it easier for me because I didn't like boys. Nobody visited me anyway, so I was indifferent to their goal of staying pure.

A lot of times I was in my own world, writing brooding poems and sob stories. In my stories, though, I usually made myself the main character with my father as the hero who would come and take me to a paradise where I would be with him forever. Sometimes I used my grandmother's tortoise tales as my background story. Sometimes I continued with the series I entitled "Questions for God." I became so obsessed with these questions for God that even in class when lessons would be going on I would be engrossed in writing poems. That never stopped, and Mr. Ogugua made me continue writing.

He would ask me to write the same poem in five different ways and show them to him when I was done. Maybe he thought he was punishing me, but I started enjoying writing. I would skip his classes and assignments with the excuse that I was busy writing the poems he told me to write. He called me one day and spoke to me about the constant image in most of my poems: my father. His recommendation was that I should use a variety of topics and images in my poetry, that I shouldn't stop including my father, but I should also work toward using other things and other people. Whenever I was sad, he would dramatize some of the poems in our textbook for me. That made me laugh a lot.

He was the one who introduced me to the debating and drama society. He turned one of my poems into a song, and we rehearsed it together before I performed it for the whole school. It was entitled "Loneliness." On the day I performed it, even though I was nervous, I felt like a star. I was one of the first and youngest students to compose and perform her poems on stage in the history of my high school. The poem was from one of my early musings, when I first started writing down my feelings and questions:

> *Loneliness, I feel the Loneliness.*
> *I am alone, alone in emptiness.*
> *Someone, someone is calling.*
> *Who can it be? Whooo, who is that calling?*
> *Is that someone me? Daddy? Daddy?*

After this performance, Mr. Ogugua enlisted me to be in the opera *The Mikado*, which aired on national television. I was a prompter, as well as a backup for Peep Bo, one of the major characters. The school's central hall was the venue for almost every activity in school. The hall was used as often as the refectory was used. We rehearsed *The Mikado* there, and also held church services and Sunday school classes there. I liked loitering around the hall sometimes even when there were no events taking place. The back of the hall gave me a rare space for privacy, especially when I wanted to be alone uninterrupted, unlike the open fields where people could run into you or see you and then run to say hello.

During one of the bible study/moral instructions, a chill ran over me. It must have been because of what was said during the bible study, so I decided to go to the back of the hall and peacefully soak in some sunlight. I had strolled around quite a bit and then had the urge to pee. I headed toward the knoll close to the side of the hall where there was less foot traffic. I took a few steps toward the hill and stumbled upon our school priest—the one who told me about the fate of Sodom and gonorrhea—cupping Chekwube's breasts and kissing her. Then he guided her hands to his bulging penis. I swung back, shaken. I peed on myself. It took me some minutes to shake off the urine trickling through my soaked underwear and down my legs. I looked around to make sure nobody saw either me or them. As if something possessed me, I tore into a race and ran into one of the empty classrooms by the left side of the school hall.

I had run into a dusty classroom with overturned chairs. Some were broken. Others were barely functional. I sat on the dusty floor and wept profusely. The scattered pieces of papers all over the floor became blurry as my tears continuously welled up and dropped into my lap like melting pebbles. They floated in and out of my sight like sea buoys. I felt as if I were drowning. I choked up as my heart heaved with a pain and burden I couldn't understand. The chaotic state of the classroom mirrored the state of my mind. I was confused. Everything in my life seemed to be caving in on me. I must have sat there for hours, but even the tolling bells for prayers didn't move me. I didn't care if one of the senior prefects or even the school principal walked in on me.

The bell for prayer came and left. Darkness enveloped me. I liked the feel of the shadows. It was calming. Except for the dimming stars of the night, I couldn't tell the difference between the darkness in the classroom and the darkness outside until stripes of moonlight slanted beams through the large window frames. I leaned firmly on the wall to get comfortable and listen to the silence around me. Only three sounds of night owls lingered in the distance.

I thought about the priest. He was the same priest who told me not to touch girls, that I would burn in hell if I continued doing so. He had told me that touching anyone's private part was a sin. He told me to wait until I got married so that my husband could do the touching as God had ordained it. Then why was he kissing Chekwube? Why did he make her massage his protruding penis? With my back still leaning on the wall, I lowered my frame and lay down, but an ant stung me, so I got up and headed to my dormitory.

To my surprise, when I arrived, Nelo was there. I had given her some space. The intensity of what I felt for her terrified me, and the constant attacks, beatings, condemnation, chastising, and judgment had overwhelmed me. So I figured a remedy would be to give some distance, seek God's face, pray, obey the priest... all lies. I looked into her eyes, as probing as they were. I didn't look away. There was concern there, and I could see the veins on her neck.

"Where have you been?" she asked, her eyes as wide as the moon.

"I was somewhere."

"Somewhere? I almost had a heart attack. I thought you had run away from school."

"I should have. Nothing makes sense to me anymore."

"What is wrong? What happened?"

I told her about the priest and the student behind our school hall. She looked shocked, but there was still doubt in her eyes. She asked me if I was sure it was the priest I saw. I told her yes, and that I was so agitated that I ran into a classroom and almost cried myself to sleep, that it was the sting of an ant that woke me up. She held me and told me it was okay. When I got settled into bed, she left.

She did daring things, like breaking the all-lights-out rule. She was supposed to be in her bed, yet she snuck out to stay in my corner. She took such risks and was never caught. I hoped that no senior prefect would see her. That would mean a harsh punishment for her for staying up late and for being outside of her dormitory so late at night. That was not the case because the next day, she came to take me with her for early morning prayers. I was shocked to see the same priest conducting the morning mass at the convent when we arrived. We had walked in as he was about to start the mass with a sign of the cross: in name of the Father, and of the Son, and of the Holy Spirit. I almost ran back.

Nelo grabbed me quickly enough and chastised me with a whisper. "Behave yourself! What is wrong?"

"That is him," I whispered back.

"That is who?"

"The priest I told you about."

"Father?"

"Yes."

She stared at him for a while as if to fish out the truth. Then she grabbed me again and said, "You are here for God, not for him."

Throughout the mass, I could barely look up at him. I didn't even dare to stand up for Holy Communion. I was shaking on my seat. The mass was barely over and I scurried out of the small chapel. I waited for Nelo outside. I was surprised when she told me I would be fine and pulled me along as she took quick steps. I didn't want to leave her side. For some reason, I became afraid of being alone. I would sleep on her comfy, secure bed because she still tied a long wrapper around the bunk bed for privacy. Most nights we told jokes, laughed and giggled.

15. Dreams and Nightmares

WHEN I WOKE up the next morning, she was staring at me, with her arms wrapped around me. "You couldn't sleep. You must have had a nightmare. You were moaning and grunting all night."

"Oh! Really? I don't even remember."

"Be calm. Everything will be all right. Okay?"

I blinked. "I hope so," I said.

She was still looking at me. This time, there was some space between us. Then she stroked my earlobes and smiled. "You are so adorable," she said.

I covered my face with both hands and laughed a stifled laugh.

"Come on, let's get ready for morning mass, and you better not say no. You need it at least for those nightmares you have. Have faith, ye woman of little faith," she said and smacked the left cheek of my buttocks. I wriggled away from her and moved to the edge of her bed.

"Don't get too comfortable. We are already late."

I reluctantly got out of bed and rushed out to brush my teeth beside the shrubs bordering her dormitory. When I got back, Diogo, one of her opposite neighbors, was arguing with her. I hurried to them, curious.

"What is going on," I asked Nelo, staring Diogo down at the same time.

"What is not wrong, when the two of you do what you do and think that nobody knows?"

"What are you babbling on about?" I asked, moving closer to her.

"How can you both fuck all night and then have the nerve to prepare for morning mass? Is that where you confess your sins?"

"You are very stupid!" I yelled and pushed her. She came close and hurled a punch at me, but I ducked. Nelo came between us and pulled me away.

"Diogo, go and report us to the highest authorityyyyyyyyy, if youuuuuuu have any evidence," Nelo stuttered. I could see a thick green vein in her neck become visible as if threatening to burst through her light, supple skin. Whenever she got really upset, she stuttered. It was my turn to hold her and pull her away. As we left the dorm, we heard Diogo's deafening voice roar through the dorm. "I do not just have evidence, I have witnesses too. *Supe* practitioners. Bloody lesbians!"

I felt a tingle of shame run down my spine, but I shook it off even though I couldn't control the goose bumps that spread all over my body. As we walked solemnly to the convent, a mild wind flirted with the edges of our pink-checked house dresses. It left a chill on my shins. Out of the blue, a flood of tears threatened to drown my eyes. I held it back by tilting my chin.

As if Nelo felt the large lump in my throat, she stopped walking and clasped my left fingers in hers. I smiled to hide the tears. She frowned but tugged me onward. A few weeks ago in my dormitory, two girls were caught having sex. It was strange because it happened in broad daylight even though their bunk bed was well covered with wrappers, so nobody could see them. However, their loud moans attracted attention. It was a bombshell because they were literally torn away from each other's naked bodies.

There was another incident where a girl was moaning, and it was discovered that she was masturbating with a candle and mistakenly got a long hunk of the candle broken and stuck in her vagina. My moaning was because of a nightmare, though. We were not doing anything wrong. Diogo's outburst was uncalled for. That was so wicked of her.

At the mass, I was able to look at the priest. I dared him to recognize my face. He didn't look my way or seem to pay any attention to the people at the mass. At intervals, we kneeled and then got up. Kneeled again and made the sign of the cross. In no time, it seemed, the mass was over and we were at the point of sharing the peace and love of Christ. We shook hands with the reverend sisters sitting next to us: "Peace be with you." The Father walked to the congregation to shake their hands in a sign of peace. I shifted as far away from him as possible. Nelo nudged me to behave myself.

After mass, we lingered. I was hoping to see Sister Kelly. Out of the corner of the chapel she came rushing toward us. Before she could make it to us, the mother superior, a plump, oily-faced woman, beckoned to her. Sister Kelly waved at us to wait. After what felt like an eternity, she eventually joined us and apologized profusely. She hugged us both and said that she hadn't seen me in a while. She accused us of always rushing out before the mass was over, and we told her we had to get ready for breakfast and do our duties before the bells caught us off guard. With a low tone, she asked us if we had ever considered joining their congregation, that she could see we loved God and devoted a portion of our time at the Blessed Sacrament. She invited us for a talk the next Sunday at the moral instructions class. We agreed to meet her there.

She was not quite out of sight when Nelo exclaimed, "Yes!"

"What are you excited about?"

"I did think about it, too. I was not sure how you would feel, though."

"What do you mean?'

"We can both join and be together. It is a safe place to be and dedicate our lives to God. We can be together and not be separated."

"Okay…" I was not sure how to feel. I was excited about the possibility of being with Nelo forever, but I was not sure that I wanted to become a reverend sister to be with her.

"That is the only way out," she insisted.

"Okay. Let me think about it," I told her. I didn't want to disappoint her with an instant no when I had not given it thorough thought. I was also struck that she thought about us being together for the long run. It was strange to me. I always thought I was alone in my dream of having a woman as my life companion. It was a secret thought I'd held close for as long as I could remember. That Nelo shared the same desire made me feel as if there was a celestial act in motion. I wouldn't have had the audacity to tell her that I wanted to share my life with her. That sounded like a crime and a sure path to the pit of hell. But here we were, thinking of our lives as one.

Before the school term was over, both Sister Kelly and the plump mother superior had started guiding us through the lives of novices. We spent more time with them in prayers, farming and serving at their kitchen. *Novice.* That was the first time I heard the word. I would find myself rolling it like chewing gum around my tongue. That was an interesting period. Not too long after, it was time for us to take the Christmas break. I wanted to spend the Christmas with Nelo at her home near Adani village, but my mother insisted I should come home, that she hadn't seen me in ages. If she had cared to see me, she would have visited me like other parents did. She just didn't want to give me the kind of liberty I was yearning for. I found that freedom in Nelo.

I had gotten used to not seeing my mother as often as I wanted. But home, when I was with her, the days went by slowly. I became agitated and restless. I missed Nelo. My mother didn't understand the sudden change in me. She teased me about how I was always eager to be with her and have her read or tell me stories.

"What happened to you?" she would ask.

I would say, "I guess I am grown now."

We would both laugh.

To preoccupy my time and distract myself from pining away for Nelo, I buried myself in books and wrote a lot of poems. I didn't do as many chores and surprisingly, my mother didn't yell at me to wash the dishes or warm up the pot of soup. Instead, she served me meals and praised me for being an "A" student.

One day, with a steaming plate of jollof rice in her hands, she looked at me and shook her head. "I am so proud of you and the scholar you have become. You don't go around looking for some wild boys to be with like our neighbor's daughter who just got pregnant a few weeks ago. You have always been a brilliant, beautiful child. I am blessed indeed. Here is some of the jollof rice I specially made for you. I also kept a bottle of Coca-Cola for you in the kitchen," she said as she dragged a small stool next to the edge of my bed to place the plate of rice.

Inasmuch as I was excited about the newfound show of affection from my mother, I was also worried about how she would feel when she discovered it was only girls I found sexually attractive. But I didn't want to think too far ahead. I returned her smile with an intermittent, "Mama daalu. Thank you." She asked me to let her know if the rice was not enough, that there was plenty in the pot. As she closed my door behind her, a weight settled on my shoulders. I was suspicious of my mother's sudden pampering. She indulged me but never in this way. I called my brother. I asked him if he knew what was going on with our mother. He was the one who gave me the clarification I needed. My mother was really shaken by the news that our neighbor's daughter, who was about my age, had gotten pregnant. I must have been about eighteen.

I thought about what might happen. I wondered if there was anybody in her family or my father's family that found their same sex attractive. I didn't want to spoil this affection. I pushed the worry away. Thoughts of Nelo flooded my mind. I was yearning for her to a near-feverish state. I wanted to see her. I had an idea of how to get to her village from the description she gave me. It seemed to be not too far away from Onitsha. I wanted to see her. I really wanted to see her. The problem was that my mother would never let me travel by myself, let alone going to see a friend who lived in another town. But I started to think about how to make the trip. My mother had mentioned that she was going to pay her mother, my grandmother, a visit at their family home at Nnebisi Road. She was going to return the next day. A day, however, wasn't going to be enough time to see Nelo. The trip would take that long, and I needed to spend time with her, even if it was for just a day.

"Mama, are you still going to see Nne?"

"Yes. Why?"

"I have not seen her in a long time. I want to go with you and spend a few days with her."

"Okay. She will be happy about that."

We set out the next day and met my grandmother gathering the eggs from her coop. She was complaining about how lizards burst the eggs and sucked the yolks, leaving her with only the shells. I hugged her from behind. She gave me a gentle squeeze after complaining that I was getting too tall and big for her squeezes. She also had a litany of questions, from my grades to my chores to my behavior. She emphasized that she hoped I behaved well and respectfully and stayed faithful to the name she gave me. Unoma: *Nwa wa mu n'uno oma*, a child born in a good home. She reminded me that she gave me the name to attract a good husband because any man who sees a lady born in a good home would know that the lady would make a good wife and a good home. "Though the oracles said otherwise, you will make a good home for your husband and your children."

"Nne, what oracle?"

I saw my mother elbow her.

"Nothing of importance, my dear."

I was eager to come up with a story to persuade my grandmother to let me go and visit my cousins at Ezennei as soon as my mother left the next day, so that I could head to Onitsha to Nelo's village. Still, I decided to spend a good part of the day with her instead to ask her what she meant by what the oracles said. It took a bit of pleading and begging before she responded, "Your mother will be mad at me. Don't let her know I told you."

"Why? Is it that bad? Tell me, Nne."

She told me that the whole family had still been trying to figure out if the soldier that held them captive cared about my mother or was taking advantage of her when my mother told her she was pregnant. She was so upset with the soldier that she had almost thought about convincing her daughter to abort the child. But a child is a child, precious, no matter the circumstances of her birth. And my mother's confession that they were both in love and had planned to ask for her blessings for their marriage stopped her in her tracks. The nine months passed surprisingly fast.

It was in the heat of the Biafra war. There were no functioning hospitals. Midwives were scarce. It was just her and her older sister who guided my mother into a thick forest to deliver me. As they dodged flying grenades and kept their eyes on the skies for bombs and explosions from artillery jets, my mother writhed in labor pain. What they had hoped would be an easy delivery became complicated. They thought my mother was not going to survive the birth. Labor pains that started at dawn lingered into the somber dusk. I was a breech baby. By the time they held my legs and pulled me out, my mother was unconscious.

There were so many complications and such chaos surrounding my life that she insisted on taking me to a traditional medicine woman to bathe me with potent herbs and look into my future for a destiny. They couldn't find any until the war subsided. When they did find one, what she told them was too shocking to accept, so they visited a second one, a man. He brought a clay bowl half-filled with water, threw about a dozen cowries into the bowl and gazed at the water to read my future. He told them the same thing: "This child will neither marry a man as a life partner, nor bear children." My grandmother said the prophet didn't want to say more. It was when they insisted that he should explain what he meant that he told them, "This child belongs to the River Goddess of Oshimili: Onishe."

They asked questions: "Is she cursed? Is she a sacrificial child? But Onishe has devotees who go on to marry and have children. Why would hers be special? Onishe can't take up all her life. She can't take up the place of a husband and children, yet you say she is not a sacrificial child? Can we cut the tie that binds them? Can we appease Onishe? Can we make sacrifices of goats and cows to appease her to let this child be? Is she a spirit child? What can we do?"

"Onishe is her guardian goddess. She is not in her life to harm her. She is a spirit child all right, but it does not end there. It is much more than that. Cutting the ties from Onishe would not change anything. She is absolute. She has not taken her life. She sustains her life."

"How? If she has not taken all of her life, why would she deprive her of the one thing that makes life worthwhile?" my grandmother had asked.

"What makes your life worthwhile may not make the life of another worthwhile. We can't all have the same path. This is her destiny, and you can't say it is not as good as any others."

At the end, sacrifices of goats and chickens were made to Onishe. I was swaddled with white cloth which was unwrapped at Onishe's shrine in exchange for yellow wads of cloth. That was to symbolize my release from Onishe's hold.

"So that took care of it?" I eagerly asked my grandmother.

"Yes. We never took you back to the river after that."

"If you take me back to the river, what would happen?"

There was a long pause before she said, "You could drown." Her response left me with the impression that she was being sarcastic, but I remembered incidents of when my mother would become hysterical when I told her I went swimming with my cousins.

She would scream at me the most and say nothing to my brother nor my cousins. My cousin Caro is a female, so it was not as if I was the only girl running around with boys. She would always call me strange names when I cackled into the showers of soothing rain. I played the longest in the rain. I lingered too long in pools of water, even in buckets. There was something nurturing about water. Could all this mean anything? There was even a time I snuck out with my cousins, Dike, Caro, and Okwudili. We had gone to River Niger to swim like most teenagers did. At first, I was apprehensive about the river until I saw my cousins swim effortlessly. Envious of their enjoyment of the river, I jumped in. That day, I drowned. They said they had panicked, that it was a group of fishermen that fished me out of the river unconscious. They pressed hard on my belly to force the water out of me. It took them a while to resuscitate me.

Eventually, they knew I had come around when I coughed out gallons of water. My cousins were terrified and begged me not to tell my mother that they invited me to the river. Everybody was shaken. They said they wouldn't have known how to tell my mother that I had drowned and died at the river. I didn't think my drowning justified my mother's fear of the river for me. It must have been a coincidence that I almost drowned. I didn't know how to swim. And if Onishe really wanted to take me, I wouldn't have survived the drowning.

My eyes settled on my grandmother's lowered gaze. She seemed to be snoring lightly. More questions weighed me down. They threatened to crush my desire to see Nelo, but my longing for her didn't stop.

We spent the rest of the afternoon and early evening with fewer words exchanged. After what seemed like a quiet, somber evening full of questions and fear, I told my grandmother that I wanted to go and spend time with my cousins at Ezennei. She offered to escort me there, but I told her I would be okay; I would return home to my mother after a couple of days. I set out for Onitsha holding tightly to the directions Nelo had written out for me on a piece of paper.

16. Apparitions and Waterlogged Terrain

A T ONITSHA, I was to take a bus to Awkuzu junction and then take a taxi to Adani. The taxi would stop at Adani market and I would see a huge cathedral. I should go to the gate of the church and ask the woman that sold oranges there where I could find the family home of the Ikwe.

The woman asked me who I was, and I told her I was Nelo's friend. She covered her tray of oranges with one of her loose wrappers and grabbed me by the hand.

"You must be a good friend to have come all the way from Asaba to visit her. That is good. Such friendships are rare. Stay close to each other, okay?"

"Yes, Ma."

There were mostly thatched houses as we walked toward a couple of cement homes in the distance, one of which had two stories. We had walked for about half a mile when I heard a piercing scream from the balcony of the two-story building, but before I could look up, the owner of the scream had disappeared. Then there was Nelo tumbling toward me as if she were a horse in a race. She almost flung me to the ground in greeting and jumped up and down, her massive bosom heaving on her chest. I had to hold her to make her stop.

She thanked the lady profusely, and then her whole family came to meet me and thanked the lady too. We went upstairs, where her three younger siblings peered at me from behind the door to their living room. Her older sister teased her about letting them get some rest now that Unoma had arrived. When I asked her sister why she'd said that, she screeched about how obsessed Nelo was with me, that she wouldn't let them drink a cup of water peacefully without her humming my name in the background.

I felt scrutinized, especially when everybody, including their father, pinned their eyes on me. As if snapped out of a trance, their mother, a tiny, dark-skinned woman, spoke up. She had been in the kitchen all the while. She asked if I was hungry and said they had some food already cooked for me. I told her I was. She hugged me and hurried out through a back door of their large living room.

I noticed that Nelo looked more like her father. He was of average height and very light-skinned. His facial expression was strange, as if he smiled and scowled intermittently. I stood by Nelo, who squeezed my hand and asked me to follow her to the room where we would be staying. It was a long room with a queen-size bed near one of the two windows, through which I could see a large expanse of a rice farm. A cluster of herons was at the edges of the farm; farther on, a couple of women seemed to be beating bags of rice. Nelo pulled me away and asked me to help her fold her clothes. She had many clothes scattered at the corner of the room. We had folded almost half of them when she rolled up one of her shirts and flung it at me. "Are you okay? You seem so quiet."

"I'm fine. I'm trying to contain the joy of seeing you again. I didn't think I would survive another week without setting my eyes on you."

"Me too. I pleaded with my dad to take me as far as Onitsha so I could find my way to you at Asaba. He scoffed and asked me to be patient till we are able to see each other again in school. It is good you came," she said and pulled me to the floor.

We were in the middle of a wrestle when her mother came in to announce that food was ready. She smiled at us. "Are you two already catching up?"

We didn't say a word. Nelo giggled and grabbed me by the waist.

The meal was a big bowl of okra soup with pounded yam. I thought it was for the two of us, but she said she was going back to the kitchen to get Nelo's plate. After the meal, we helped ourselves to bottles of malt drink and then caught up on how I made my way from Asaba. Nelo's father seemed impressed that I was able to come all the way by myself. He asked me why I arrived late and said I should have set out earlier in the morning. I told him it was not too far and it had been quite easy to find them. I also told him that there were a couple of fellow travelers who were headed to nearby villages.

He asked more questions. I told him about one of the travelers who was an agricultural extension officer on his way to inspect some rice farms, and about another lady who was going to Onitsha to sell her fish. He patted my back and told me that I was a determined girl. He smiled, but then that scowl settled again on his face before he left the room. I just stared at my toes until Nelo suggested we go back to the room because we had a lot to catch up on.

As we sat on the bed, she asked me what I did at home. While we were on holiday she was bored most of the time. I told her I was also bored, but that I tried to read and sleep when I was not daydreaming about her. She pulled me close to her and made faces at me. We both laughed hysterically and then lay on the floor, staring at the ceiling. A wave of cold from the concrete slab made me pull the blanket closer around me.

I heard Nelo's voice. It was faint. I opened my eyes, and she was standing over me. She was just in her underwear and a loose white shirt. "You dozed off," I heard her say. I was still a bit groggy. Then she kneeled beside me and circled me with her arms as if to lift me.

"You can't! You can't lift me. I don't know what you think you are, Super Woman?" I laughed.

"Let's see," she said and grunted in an effort to lift me. I leaped up, and she chased me around the room until I was out of breath and she caught me. She held me from behind as we both stared out through the window. Except for shafts of faint light that flooded into the room, everywhere was dark already. The air was warm, and trills of crickets overwhelmed the night.

In bed, we could barely see each other's faces. Nelo asked if I was cold or warm. I told her I was comfortable; she snuggled up to me. The air around us felt tense. She was so beautiful. The soft feel of her body made my breathing shallow. Her dreamy eyes were like ponds I yearned to submerge myself in. When she looked at me, my heart skipped boisterously. We stared at each other and then kissed. A strong surge of sweet sensation rushed down my spine. I cradled her face in my hands.

At first, our kissing was gentle. It gradually built up to a faster tempo until we pulled off our clothes. I buried my face in her belly, rolled my tongue in the groove of her belly button and then walked my way up to her large, supple breasts. Her nipples were turgid, and I sucked on one of them, and then pulled them together to suck on both at the same time. She moaned and found my face with her tongue. We kissed as we groped for our groins. I pushed her down and thrust my thigh between her legs, teasing her lips with the tip of my tongue. The night faded. The rings of crickets were like music that rose with the rhythm of our bodies until it reached a crescendo that found us wailing and yelping in each other's arms with an unfathomable surge of pleasure. We involuntarily reached for each other's mouths, but it was too late. The door swung open. It was her father.

"Are you both okay?" he asked. The flame of his handheld lamp flickered and flapped from the window breeze. His face seemed distorted in the broken light.

"We are fine. Nelo was having a bad dream," I lied, trying to slow my breathing.

He lowered his frame over Nelo, who pulled the blanket closer around her neck and assured him she was okay.

"You are both sweating," he said and glanced at me as he tried to wipe the sweat off Nelo's face with the edge of his long-sleeved shirt. "Let me open up the other windows."

They were already open. He came back to check on Nelo one last time before he left. I think I heard him whisper "good night" when he shut the door behind him. We looked at each other with our mouths wide open. Without saying a word, we clung to each other.

When I heard Nelo's gentle breathing, I stared at the window. It was a star-studded night. The sounds of the crickets had subsided. Frogs, instead, were croaking. I was not sure how I felt. For some reason, I had an intense urge to cry, yet there was a deep joy in my heart. I ended up weeping. I could feel myself shaking as the tears trickled down and soaked the pillow, but I tried to hold myself so as not to wake Nelo. She woke up anyway and held me. She didn't ask me why I was crying. She just told me in her usual comforting tone it was going to be okay and placed my face on her bosom as she kissed my forehead.

We slept for a long time because when we woke up, it was almost noon and Nelo's family was nowhere to be found. She didn't seem worried. She said they had gone to morning mass, and from there they would visit some relatives and friends. The sun was fierce, and I had a sudden urge to go outside for some air. We stood on the balcony of their two-story building and took in the stretch of traffic. Some people were on their way to the stream. Others straddled huge baskets and bags on their way to the market. I asked if we could visit the stream, if it was nearby, and Nelo said we would when her family got back. She also told me to get ready for an evening mass since we'd missed the morning one.

At the stream, I was surprised to see how filled it was. Children, men, and women were there. Some were swimming. The women were mostly washing while children played and splashed one another. I stood beside the stream and watched with keen interest.

At Asaba, there were not so many people gathered at the same time at the river. Maybe it was because we had a river and there was enough space for everyone to spread. Nelo watched me, laughing. She asked me why I wanted to come to the stream when I didn't even as much as want to touch the water. I scurried to the stream and scooped some water and threw it at her. She ran off. I stepped up to the dry land and wandered around the stream while she trailed me. I stumbled upon a small mud house with an entrance that had sprinkles of chicken feathers and white pieces of cloth tied around a leaf-filled clay pot. She told me it was a shrine for those who worshipped the stream god. I shivered at the sight of the shrine because it triggered strange images that occasionally invaded my dreams. They came in patches of phantasmagorias, but the dreams and scene were consistent.

That night in Nelo's arms, I had the dream again.

It was dawn. Mating insects perched at the edges of shrubs that flanked one side of the river. I stood beside a pool that had formed, an estuary of the river. There were ripples on top. I held firm to the fowl in my hand. When the ripples seemed to have disappeared, I waded into the river and felt the knotted end of my white wrapper above my breasts and blinked my white-chalked eyes. I returned my knife to my hand and held the white rooster more firmly, waiting until I felt the presence of the river goddess. I dipped the rooster into the lake. With a gulping sound,

I raised it. Trails of water ran down its damp feathers into the river. I watched them fall, drop by drop, and the rooster began to shudder. Its eyes were shut, and it flapped its head to snap out water through its nostrils with a noise like a hiccup.

I called out to the goddess to see the sacrifice for the cleansing then struck the neck of the rooster. It convulsed. Blood gushed out, and its head fell into the water. A flow of blood streamed into the river, dark, thinning clouds. I called the goddess again and lifted the rooster. *Here is the sacrifice*, I said. *You watch over our land and mortals do go to slumber. In slumber, the strangers' footsteps never stirred them. They are mortals, great goddess.*

The goddess rose from the edge of the river as if coming up from a dive and sat calmly on the water in a lotus position, floating. She was small but with enormous breasts. Her skin was dark and glossy. She had long dreadlocks. Her huge breasts covered her lap. I looked at her too-familiar face, but her features were blurred. I could only make out the oval outline. Then the water wobbled and she descended. I placed the dead rooster in her shrine and sat awhile on a patch of grassy, dried mud beside the river. When I had rested, I walked back to the river, washed my hands, took a bath and surveyed that portion of the river before I went home.

***

When I woke up, I felt awkward. I didn't want to tell Nelo about the dream as I had never mentioned it to anyone. I always brushed it off. It was just a dream. We talked about our plans and our lives. She brought up the need for us to consider joining the convent to become reverend sisters again.

"I want to give my life to God," she said solemnly. "We can do it together. Call it our escape." She dug her fingers into my short Afro.

"What are we escaping from?" I asked, pinching her hand.

"The world." She laughed and pinched back, but she pulled away before I could reach out for another pinch. I told her I needed more time to think about it. Inasmuch as I would be the happiest person on earth if there was a way we could spend the rest of our lives together, I wondered what I would do to achieve that.

The next day, I was ready to return to Asaba. Nelo almost created a scene with her tears. Her dream eyes were red, and I promised her that since I knew the way to her place I would visit often, especially when we were on holidays. She nodded as I wiped the snot from her nose with my handkerchief. Her whole family saw me off to the motor park, and her father gave me money and paid my fare.

As the rickety Toyota car raced past massive elephant grasses, I prayed that my mother hadn't found out I was not in Asaba. I figured she would be calm knowing I was with my grandmother. I got into Asaba just before four p.m. and snuck into my grandmother's house. As usual, she was cleaning out her chicken coop when I slid past her. She was surprised to see me. "I thought you went home to your mother."

"No, Nne. I told you I was going to spend some time with my cousins at Ezennei."

"Oh, yes. You did say so. How are they doing?"

"They are fine. I should be going home now."

"You can spend one more day with me. No?"

I turned down her suggestion with the promise that I would visit her again soon. She offered to walk me through Ogbeilo past the Odua and Ofia family homes. As we passed each one, she told me how the family was related to us. She walked me down to Ogwa-ahaba and then to the path toward St. Patrick's College before she bid me goodbye.

When I got home, my mother was cooking nsala soup. It was one of my favorites, especially when she stuffed the soup with fresh fish. She didn't seem to have missed me. Instantly, she asked me to blow some life into the dying embers of the firewood. I bent down near the smoky firewood and blew with my mouth. I would have kept blowing except that she kept staring at me. My mother said a lot and did a lot with her eyes. When I caught the smoldering anger there, I ran into the house to get the raffia fan she usually asked me to use. I didn't know why I didn't think about that.

That she didn't ask me why I stayed away for a couple of days was surprising. I was really trying hard to please her and distract her from anything I could do to betray myself—even if it meant being down on my knees and blowing the dying embers of smoke-choked wood with my mouth. I fanned for what seemed an endless hour before the yellow flames burst into life. The soup bubbled. I made my way to the large spoon she had placed in a plate beside the tripod fire and took a lick of the spoon. I was about to stir the soup when her eyes fell upon me again. I rinsed it out before stirring the soup.

"Enough! Before you break the fish into bits," she said and snatched the spoon away from me. "Itchy throat! Always sniffing around for what to lick or eat."

"Is she no longer your scholar?" Out of nowhere, my sister appeared. I ran up to hug her but then realized she was wobbling with a huge bucket of water on her head. I was pleasantly surprised to see her because she spent most of her time in school or with her friends in other towns. I hoped she didn't stay long enough to get on my nerves as she typically did. The water was spilling and splashing all over her body as her lean frame shook to the sway of the bucket. My mother helped her put it down, but she wouldn't shut up. "Where did you wander off to, leaving everything for me to do as usual?"

"Let her be," my mother interjected.

"You spoil her and then you think there is a man out there who would want to marry her lazy self? She can't wash. She can't cook, and she can't clean. She will never find a husband."

"I see you missed me," I told her.

"Who missed you with your big head? I see you have added half an inch to your height. That is good."

My mother let our argument continue without a word, and when she finally said something, she asked me to grab a bucket and follow her to get more water.

For some reason, thoughts of Nelo didn't preoccupy my mind as they had before I visited her.

17. Monsoon Winds

WHEN SCHOOL RESUMED, it was the first time my mother came with me to Nsukka. She had bought a lot of provisions like powdered milk, Cabin biscuits, canned fish, corn flakes, sugar, and a sizable bag of garri. I wanted her to meet Nelo. They warmed up to each other right away.

Nelo kept saying I looked like my mother. We probably had the same complexion and the same face, but I insisted that the resemblance was not much. I also wanted my mother to meet Sister Kelly and the mother superior of our convent, but she frowned and said she would see them next time. She had sternly warned me not to think about becoming a reverend sister when I brought up the topic after visiting Nelo. She had said she wouldn't encourage the idea, and I had shrugged off her warning. If that was what Nelo wanted, then I was going to join the congregation of the Holy Rosary with her.

One Saturday morning after most of us were done with the chores of cleaning out our corners, washing, and completing our dormitory tasks, a bunch of girls invited me to go to the cashew orchards a few miles away from our school. Nobody was paying attention. Everyone was carefree. I jumped at the invitation.

In no time, we walked past an isolated federal hospital at Ede Obala and then took a foot-worn path to burst into the cashew field. We ate as much as we could and stuffed our plastic bags with as many cashews as would fit. Our uniforms were stained with cashew nut oil. It was difficult to wash of cashew stains, but

I didn't care. I was no longer hungry, and it was an adventure I enjoyed. We hurried back to school with wide grins. I was eager to see Nelo and give her some of the cashews.

The reception I got from her was not expected. She was livid. She repeatedly asked me why I would join a group of wild girls in the bush for cashews as if I had never eaten in my whole life. Between confusion and agitation, my jaw dropped. There had to be something else that was making her so angry. While she kept yelling at me, some students who were passing by came to ask for some cashews.

"If this is what is making you so angry, I will throw them away. Would that make you feel better?" The students kept coming, as if they were oblivious to the tension surrounding us.

"It's not about the cashews," Nelo yelled back. "It is about you not telling me where you were going, and to make matters worse, you left with these unruly girls to pick wild cashews. We have food in the locker, so what could have been your reason?"

Her voice was almost drowned out by the incessant begging of the girls. Out of frustration for her anger and the irritating voices of the beggars, I flung the bag of cashew nuts to the floor and told them to have it all. As if making a mockery of our fight, they lingered asking if I meant that they could have all of the nuts. When I said yes, they still asked, "Are you sure?"

"Yes! Yes! All of it. Take!" I screamed at the top of my voice.

For a minute, Nelo was silent until she saw the patches of cashew oil on my dress. She opened her mouth to say something, then closed it. Then she stomped away, shaking her head. I hurried after her and followed her to her corner in the dormitory. That was our first fight, and I was terrified I was going to lose her. Once I apologized, she forgave me and made me promise I would not go cashew hunting again. I promised, though I couldn't understand why she wanted to control what I did and where I went.

I continued cashew hunting because I enjoyed the adventure and the cashews. Almost all she did was stay in her corner, go to prayers and talk about being in the religious life. I liked listening and sharing my thoughts with her, but I didn't want to do all that as an everyday routine. So my hunts for cashews didn't end. All I did was make sure she never found out.

A few weeks later, school was abuzz with multiple events. I concentrated on rehearsing for *The Mikado*. There were a number of debates lined up for our debating society too. These kept me busy even though Nelo and I were scheduled for more novice-life practice. Nelo became more demanding of my time. It was a good thing that we were in *The Mikado* together. With constant rehearsals, I made a lot of beautiful and brilliant friends: Ukamaka, Golum, Chinwe, Chinelo, Tayo, Elizabeth, Ifeoma, and many others. They were all my seniors but we had a strong connection. There was lots to talk about from sciences to the arts. They were all exceptionally clever.

One of my most memorable times as a teenager was when Ukamaka came to visit me at my uncle's house at UNN. She had come in a shiny Benz and was ushered out by her driver. I think my cousins and my aunt were astonished to see her and maybe surprised that I could have such an elite visitor. What I kept hearing in the background of our home was, "Who is that? Who is she looking for?" I was not sure about inviting her to sit in our sparkling living room. Nobody was allowed to sit there except older visitors. The only time I stepped onto the carpet or dared touch the seats was when I was either sweeping or dusting them. So I ran out to welcome her and then invited her to sit with me in the sofa that was in our porch—it was my turn to be shocked when my aunt invited her in to sit in the living room. I hovered over her, unsure whether I had attained the right to sit in the sacred space. I was not only asked to sit, we were served snacks and drinks together. That did something to my self-esteem; it soared.

At school, we became even closer. Then there were rumors that we were lovers, but we were not fazed by that. As she was a senior, nobody could as much as bully me about our friendship. So it felt like I enjoyed a certain protection from their status as seniors. Thanks to *The Mikado*. In no time, Ukamaka's set was ready to graduate, but my friendship with most of the cast members progressed beyond the walls of our school.

The seasons at Queens tarried. Bells. Prayers. Mass. Life continued in its rhythm, but the harmattan wind of that year came with a peculiar cold. We were reluctant to take cold baths. Electric sockets kept burning out or exploding. We boiled water to bathe or carried on without baths. We were getting close to taking our West African Examination Council Exam (WAEC), and its approach got us into more intrigue and covert plans on how to get cheat papers and answers before the exam day. We lost our money even as we burned more night candles studying. The officers in charge of the WAEC papers were to wait at Enugu where the answers would be dropped from the air and then delivered to us. We were to pay twenty naira each. I dared not mention it to Nelo. I knew she would be mad at me. I was worried and desperate to pass math. I hated it.

Math was one of the papers that was to be dropped for us at Enugu. We had made plans with some boys from St. Theresa's College. They were to meet us at the remote end of our school fence to drop the papers. We waited for days. Our pockets were emptied. No plane landed. No boy came to deliver the papers. In the frantic last days before the math exam, I pleaded with Nelo to teach me. She did her best, but math still remained elusive. They were meaningless figures that jumped around on the page. I failed it. Luckily, UNN, where I had gained admission to study English, only required a credit in any science subject. Math was not one of the mandatory courses for admission into an undergraduate program.

Even when the first set of subjects were taken, we were still waiting for the papers we paid for. The boys from town and from St. Theresa's College regaled us with stories of how special police forces mounted barbed wires to retrieve the papers from the plane. The stories were endless. Some still had faith, borrowed money and waited for papers that never arrived. Unexpectedly somebody told Nelo that I was involved in a school racket. At first, she stopped speaking to me. Then she decided to talk to me about it. Because she didn't come off as angry, I was confused. When I asked her why she was so calm about it, she said she had realized that anger or screaming at me didn't do anything. We then started a marathon math session.

As much practice as we had, I couldn't concentrate. It was either her dreamy eyes or her gentle gestures. When I wouldn't stop being a clown by either kissing her shoulders or stroking her hand, she yelled at me with a stutter. I felt bad and stopped. All her efforts seemed futile because when she gave me some math tests to practice with, I failed all the questions. I accepted my fate and resorted to finding ways to sit next to a girl who was good at math. Unfortunately, seats were assigned. Seated during the exam, I asked the girl sitting next to me if she was good at math. She was. I pleaded with her to let me copy her answers. I thought I copied quite well, but nothing in her paper made sense. I was not sure about there to put the dots and the fractions. It was no surprise when the results came out and I'd failed.

As the semester drew to a close, I became restless and apprehensive. I was afraid of losing everything I had nurtured and built up in six long years. Nelo and I had decided to firm up our plans and work out our exit from school life and into the walls of a convent. In the last days, as the term ground to its final halt, we were inseparable. At some point, I moved most of my things to her dormitory. I was now a senior and didn't care what anybody said to me.

As if the impending "end" was not hard enough, our WAEC results were released, and I had a mere pass, a P7, which was a couple of points away from an F, fail, in English. It was a shock I could not contain. I was one of the best graduating students in English and Literature. I took pride in being one of the pioneer editors for our high school magazine. Even our principal, Mrs. Eze, was shaken. She took it upon herself to have WAEC accept a special request to regrade my English paper. But it was going to take another year for another round of re-marks.

I watched my life cave in. I had already been accepted by the University of Nigeria to study English. Between not knowing what would become of my relationship with Nelo and the uncertainties of undergraduate studies, I wanted nothing more than to die. No amount of consolation from anyone was good enough. The principal suggested I stay back in school, that she would give me a special room, and I would live as regular students did. I turned down the offer even when Nelo said she'd stay with me. She had applied to study optometry but was offered veterinary medicine instead. She decided to take the Joint Admission Matriculation Board Examination and try for medicine again.

In the end, my uncle was able to work out something for me. He enrolled me in the archaeology department while I waited for my English to be re-marked. Archaeology didn't require a credit in English. A P7 was good enough.

The positive news didn't brighten up my cloudy mood. Students ran helter-skelter, packing up their things while their parents patiently waited. I stood in the middle of my dormitory wondering what was to become of me. It was as if I were in the middle of a whirlwind. In my mind, everything was spinning out of control, but I was rooted, motionless. Nelo knew how to reach out to me in overwhelming moments. When she approached me, I was half in tears.

"We can leave tomorrow. My dad can drop you off at your uncle's house on campus. Or you can come home with me till UNN starts in May," she said and held me. I pulled away from her to gather what was left of my belongings and followed her outside, where the wind was chilly though light. The school looked like a war zone. Students were still running around, bumping into each other and screaming out their goodbyes.

18. Shallow Land

IN 1988, I was fresh from high school, admitted to the University of Nigeria, Nsukka. My first day at UNN was cold. I felt like a chicken stripped of all its feathers. Any warmth I had preserved felt plucked away. I had a strong feeling that my life there was going to be personified in the saying that a rolling stone gathers no moss. In my case, there were no roots and nothing to hold me firm. Wide-eyed, I stepped with caution. My hostel was Okpara Hall. My roommate was a self-professed born-again Christian.

The English department became a home of sorts for me. I discovered poetry again there because there was a prominent departmental board where poetry lovers and poets stuck their poems for comments. Alienated and depressed half of the time, I drowned myself in books and poetry writing. With time, I made friends with some girls from high school I stumbled upon in my department. Frequent visits to one another's rooms were exciting initially. However, I discovered they were more interested in men than poetry and reading. I started withdrawing from them until I was able to completely cut off from them. That was the norm. There was nothing wrong with that. It was just unfortunate that I couldn't relate to them on that level.

I was in my room one day, daydreaming—though I was occasionally brought back to reality with my roommate's aggressive prayers—when I heard an angelic voice. The hymn soared down the hallway. *Who is this person?* I wondered and leaped out of my bed and hurriedly opened my door. I followed the trail of the voice. It was a shapely back with swinging hips that my eyes fell upon. She was gracefully stepping down the stairs of our toilet area. I held my breath, hoping that she wouldn't slip and fall on our constantly wet toilet end stairways. She didn't fall. I decided to wait. She must have gone there to throw out some water.

In no time, she gingerly walked up the same stairs and continued the song. She stopped when she noticed that I was smiling at her. She smiled back, and her almond face brightened. I introduced myself and asked for her room number. Her name was Ng. She pointed at her room with a chuckle. Her large eyes became even wider. Her room was a couple of doors away from mine. I followed her to her room. When we got to the door, she stepped aside for me to enter, demonstrating that I go in first. "Be my guest," she said. There was something about her that I was already beginning to like.

Ng apologized for the wet floor next to her bed. She was washing. I told her it was okay, but instantly she was on her knees cleaning out the water. When she was done, she asked if I would like some peanuts and banana. My heart was warming up. I really liked her. She told me she wanted to be a doctor but wanted to get a degree in microbiology first. She asked what I was studying and what I wanted to pursue as a career. I didn't know what to tell her. I knew I loved writing, but who makes a career of writing?

"Journalism," I said, and she smiled her big-eyed smile again. She announced that she had a class and would soon head out. "Of course!" I told her. "See you again soon."

"At least you know my room now. You can always visit," she said.

"Likewise," I said, grabbed her hand and squeezed it. I knew it may have been too quick, but I found her attractive and hoped we could get close. It was futile for me to think that she could possibly find women attractive like me. That would be pushing it too far.

I was hopeful yet. Part of the process of finding out if somebody was gay was frustrating. It felt like throwing out bait and hoping that whoever I was talking to would catch it. Otherwise, it would be a long, drawn-out process of dropping hints here and there. Often, the attempts ended up being a waste of time. Frustrated or defeated, I would tuck my tail between my legs, like a beaten dog, and crawl back to my hole. It took a lot of caution and a lot of trial and error with the hope that one would not be found out and disgraced. Being open enough to let anyone know I was a lesbian came at a great cost. I lived most of my days there and a large number of my years at Queens invisible.

By the time I left Ng and got to my room, my roommate had locked me out. I didn't have my keys. I screamed out her name in case she was in the toilet. No response. I walked down the stairs toward the toilet. The stench was unbearable, so I walked back to my room, knocked on the door. No answer. I walked to the entrance of my hostel and lingered there for a while until it occurred to me to go to a classmate's room where I could stay until nighttime when my roommate might return. She was not in her room.

I resorted to lingering at the entrance of my hostel where pretty and skimpily dressed girls waltzed in and out. It was quite a feast for my eyes. I hadn't realized how hard and long I had been staring at a tall, model-like girl until she turned around to make clear she had noticed me. I smiled at her, but she rolled her eyes and hurried off. I wondered what her problem was. I was merely looking. Who does looking hurt? I hissed at her swinging backside. I did feel like a clown, though. I knew I was lusting after them. I missed Nelo. She would have saved me all these troubles if she were here. We had agreed on visits. She had to do most of them since she was still at home, and while I waited for her visits to come around, I felt free to admire other women. My intention was not to get into full-blown affairs; that seemed like a far-fetched fantasy, I planned to follow as my heart led while taking it one day at a time.

Darkness gradually crept in, and streetlights came on even as pop and party music blasted through the windows of Okpara Hall. I decided to check my mail which was right next to the main entrance before I took a long walk. There, in my mailbox, was Nelo's mail. I stuffed it into my jeans pocket and walked toward St. Peter's Cathedral. As I looked up at the towering cross on top of the church building, nostalgia came over me: morning masses, tending to piglets, pruning pineapples in orchards, constant kneeling that hardened my knees. I desired a religious life, but I was terrified of being among women. I did not trust myself enough to focus on a calling. I didn't want to fail God. I could try, maybe.

I grimaced and a bird flapped by. I walked up the hill to the restaurant area called Hill-top, except that I had no money for food. Up on the rugged path of Hill-top, the aroma of egusi and tomato stew teased my nostrils. I eagerly searched every eating space with a craned neck. It was hard to see, even though the torn, swaying curtains of the restaurants intermittently parted wide enough to give me a good view of the people inside. There was nobody I knew. I kept a straight face. After a few more minutes of an uphill walk, I made my way toward my hostel. I decided to walk into the church and whisper a prayer.

As I sat, I felt the crunch of Nelo's letter. The feeling of nostalgia became even stronger, especially when she wrote repeatedly in one sentence that she missed me and might be visiting soon to see me and her sister, who was also a student at UNN. I was surprised because she had never mentioned it. I thought about it a second time, and it occurred to me that her sister, like her father, didn't quite approve of our relationship. She never openly condemned it, but she always shook her head at us with a smirk. Maybe Nelo wanted to keep me away from the subtle hostility.

I was still pondering why she might not have wanted me to meet her sister when an altar boy walked up and placed some candles on the altar table. I got up and left. I was in no mood for mass.

My roommate was not yet back, so I stood on one of the pavements that hedged our hostel from the parking lot out front and leaned on the building while I watched people go by. I found my eyes drifting to butts of well-endowed girls. At least darkness shielded me. Girls trooped out of the hostel with their plates to buy dinner from a cluster of "mama puts" that usually arrived in the evenings. As they lined up for their turns, more food hawkers settled in their corners. A while later, when it got too dark for me to see the full outline of women's shapes, I decided to check if Ng was back from her classes. She was in her room chattering with a bunch of men. I had opened the door before I heard their voices, and I made to retreat, hoping that she wouldn't see me, but she yelled out my name and asked me to come and meet her classmates. That was a relief. I did wonder if she had a boyfriend. They were just her classmates.

The conversation was about lecturers and how difficult they could be and how they exploited students by forcing them to buy their handouts. Our talk seemed interesting until they invited me for a Christian fellowship. Before I could give them a response, they pulled out some tracts from their old-fashioned briefcases. I thanked them and told them I would come if Ng agreed to come with me. They asked her to make sure she brought me to the fellowship. She scoffed and said she would, after which they got up and asked to be escorted out. We escorted them all the way to the art theater and then turned around. We were almost back at our hostel when Ng pulled me to sit down with her on the chair students called "Lover's Bench." She said she wanted to take in some fresh air before she returned to her stuffy room where her roommate never turned off her stove.

We sat there until the moon appeared. Its sight was enthralling. There was a romantic air, but maybe it was in my mind because I had already started stringing some poetic sentences in my head. I slid my hand into hers, and she gave me a firm squeeze. She teased me about how soft and little my fingers were. As she turned, the moonbeams cast a silhouette of her frame across my chest, and her laughter was a piece of beautiful song. She was from Enugu, the oldest of five children, and she had to pave the way for her sisters to follow. That was why she wanted to be a doctor. It was considered a prestigious profession in her family.

While we were seated on the Lovers' Bench, deep in conversation in the middle of a calm and warm evening, two student evangelists interrupted our conversation and asked if we had given our lives to Christ. They also asked us if we were waiting for wayward campus boys to use us for their October Rush, which was a term used to describe the habit of older male students who preyed on the naivety of freshman female students for sex. When we didn't respond they asked if we were waiting for married men to pick us up. We still ignored them, and they brought out their bibles and talked about how the world was coming to an end when young girls freely gave their bodies away to strange men who would never marry them.

I got up and nudged Ng, but she said we should hear them out. We listened as they wailed about how we should save our lives before it was too late. We agreed. Then they asked which hostel we lived in so they could come and visit us for a follow-up. I looked away. It seemed as if the more tolerant we were, the more aggressive they became. For them to leave, I gave them the wrong hostel and the wrong room number. The name I gave them was Slessor Hall, which was the female hostel right behind where we were sitting. Ng did the same, and we giggled as they left.

By the time we got to our hostel, my roommate was back. She didn't seem to care when I told her that she locked me out.

She just grunted and flung herself on her bed. A round of loud snoring made it obvious that she had dozed off, which was a good thing because then I could play the cassette I had been wanting to listen to through my headphones. Her not interrupting with loud prayers was a sweet relief. Ng had gone to meet her study group at our neighboring female hostel, Balewa. I found myself thinking about her quite a bit. I didn't know if I should tell her that I really liked her or just let our friendship blossom. I decided to tell her.

The next day, after my lectures, I went to her room and saw her in an awkward position with a lanky, gap-toothed guy. Her left leg was flung across his right leg and they seemed to be gazing into each other's eyes. I frowned and made to duck back to the door, but she called out my name.

"Unoma!"

"Sorry, I didn't mean to disturb you guys."

"You're not disturbing anything. Come and meet my cousin, Emeka."

"Phew!" Relief. "Hello, Emeka. Nice to meet you," I said and stretched out my hand for a handshake.

"I don't give girls handshakes," he said and reached out to hug me. Hesitantly, I leaned in with the edge of my right shoulder. He rattled on about how pretty I was and how he must have seen me around the drama department. I told him it was possible because I had friends there. He kept talking on and on, and I bore it because of Ng. Eventually, he got up to go. We escorted him all the way to the same art building we were at the previous night.

As we bade him goodbye and walked toward our hostel, Ng grabbed my hand. That gave me the courage to speak up. "I want to tell you something."

"What?" she asked, looking hard at me.

"I like you."

"I like you too, and is that not why we are friends? If I didn't like you, we wouldn't be friends."

"I mean that I really, really like you."

"I don't understand," she said and cleared her throat. "But I like you too." Confusion settled on her face. "Is there a different way to like a friend?"

"It's okay. It's good to know that you like me too." I struggled inside. I was afraid to let her know that I wanted more than a friendship. If a deeper relationship with her were possible, it would merely be an affair. I wouldn't imagine that any woman would entertain the idea of a long-term relationship with a woman at UNN. So I didn't feel so guilty about cheating on Nelo. My relationship with her was for life. I wanted to open up to Ng, but I also didn't want to scare her away. I decided to wait a while before telling her that I wanted more than friendship. Maybe the right occasion would present itself.

One day at my department, I bumped into my old high school buddies. They asked me where I had been. I didn't want to tell them that I decided to stop spending time with them because all they talked about were boys or men and makeup. I told them that I was out of town for a while. One of them said that we had the same classes and that she often saw me in class. I lied that I often left for town after my lectures. They invited me to a party they planned to throw over the weekend and promised me there would be plenty of fine boys and good food. I told them I would come for the food, not the boys. One of the girls, Nkadi, pulled me to the side and asked, "Do you already have a boyfriend?"

"No."

"Then why don't you come for this party? There is a cute guy I will introduce you to."

"I am not interested."

"Why? Don't tell me you are still into *supe* and doing girls. That was then, in the past. We did it because there were no boys. There are plenty of boys now, so you have no excuse."

For some reason, my throat tightened. I found myself being upset. "I don't like boys," I told her.

"See, what we did in secondary school was a phase. It is in the past. It is gone. Besides, how do you even know that you are not into boys when you have not even tried dating a guy?"

"Do I need to date one before I know I don't like them in that way?"

"Yes."

"I have heard," I said and started walking away.

"At least come to the party for the food, if not the fine guys," she said loudly.

I hurried my steps toward my hostel. I checked Ng's room, but she was not there. My roommate's smoky little stove did not help matters. My eyes stung from the smoke. I wanted to run away from her, from Nkadi, from the school and the stupid so-called fine guys. When the smoke became unbearable, I left the room.

"Sorry, oh! I am almost done cooking," I heard her say.

I stood outside for some fresh air and steadied my frame on the concrete slab in front of my hostel: one of my usual spots to ogle girls. It was an isolated area. The shadow of darkness kept me out of sight as I indulged in my hobby. Most of them were coupled with guys. I was also looking out for Ng. I waited outside long enough for my roommate to have finished her cooking. Before I entered my room, I checked on Ng again. She was not there. I was beginning to worry, but my anxiety was soothed by the steamy plate of rice my roommate offered me. She'd made the stew with geisha—canned mackerel fish—since she couldn't find fresh fish and tomatoes, she explained. I didn't care. I was too hungry.

19. A Ball of Cactus, Rolling

IT HAD BEEN two days and Ng was still nowhere to be found. I got tired of reading and listening to music, so I decided to go to the party Nkadi invited me to. By the time I got there, her room was full of people. There was barely any space to sit. As soon as she saw me, she called out my name and dragged me to the edge of her bed and told the guys sitting on the bed to make space for me. They did. Then she whispered something into the ears of a light-skinned, bulky guy. The guy smiled at me and asked if I wanted something to drink. I found that strange since it was not his party.

"Maybe later, not now," I said.

"Okay. Let me know when."

I had hoped that Nkadi was not trying to hook me up with a dude that looked like Hulk. When I confronted her about it a few hours into the party, she denied trying to hook me up. She said that the guy she had in mind had not shown up. In my mind, I knew she was crazy for taking it upon herself to find me a boyfriend. I was trying to hurry up and get some food, eat, and leave when an average-height guy with very low-cut hair shuffled in. He started bumping to MC Hammer's "Can't Touch This." He mimed it as he swung around in a frenzy. It was a cue for me to leave, but I didn't want to stuff my food and there were no takeaway plates in the room.

The dancing guy sat down and asked Nkadi to bring his food and drink. Before Nkadi would respond, he leaped up to the sound of Ace of Base's "All That She Wants." I smiled at his silly dance steps. I was polishing off the last bit of rice and moi-moi when Nkadi lowered the volume of her music and introduced us. His name was Victor. He said he was also in the English department but couldn't remember seeing me. I used the same excuse of how I usually left immediately after my lectures and told him that now I knew his face, I would be on the lookout for him. He asked me for my hostel and my room number.

Just as I was about to give him the wrong hostel and some random room number, TLC's "No Scrubs," came on. I found myself laughing at the words and the coincidence of the lyrics. "No," kept ringing in my head. "No." "No." He asked me why I was laughing. Before I could respond, he pulled me to the dance floor and started dancing while I stood on the spot still laughing. So as not to cause a scene, I moved along with the rhythm of the music. He said I was a fine girl as he gently swayed back and forth. For the first time, I noticed his thick Igbo accent. I was ready to go but he begged me to stay.

At the end of the party close to midnight, I was still feeling stuffed even with all the dancing Victor was so determined to do. He offered to take me safely to my hostel. I told him not to worry. He insisted. We ended up at Slessor. I thanked him and disappeared into a corner of the hall. After waiting for what seemed like an eternity, I came out to peek around and make sure he was not in sight. Then I scuttled toward the school refectory, wound my way to Balewa Hall and then my hostel, Okpara.

Victor was the one person I was not looking forward to seeing on Monday morning inside the English department general office. He asked me why I ran away from him and why I didn't want him to know my room. When I said nothing, he said he would not force me to be his friend. He opened a black briefcase and pulled out a wad of papers with scribbling on them.

"These are some of my poems I want you to read and critique. Nkadi said you are a poet too. Maybe we can exchange poems and critique each other," he said pleadingly.

I took the pages and told him that I posted some of mine on the department's information board.

He seemed surprised. "You wrote 'Probings'?"

"Yes. Why do you look surprised?"

"I didn't know that a girl as little as you could write like that."

"Okay. Thank you."

In no time, we became friends. When Ng seemed too busy with her studies, Victor was a fair alternative, especially because we read and discussed mostly poetry. Our poetry sessions were going well until he invited me to his room. He had said that he organized a poetry reading in his room if I wanted to come. I told him that I would think about it. Eventually, I went to his hostel because he insisted that since I didn't want him to know my hostel I should come and know his.

As we stepped into his hostel, Mbanefo Hall, there was a bunch of boys making catcalls. I was uneasy. He told me to ignore them. But the cackle became even louder, so he shouted at the boys to shut it. That made it worse. I tried to cover my face. That didn't help. We hastened to his room, and he slammed the door on all the commotion. I asked him why they did that. He said that they were just being stupid because they didn't usually see girls in their dormitory, so when they did see one, they got excited. His explanation was not convincing. My impression was that because they thought every girl that visited came for sex, they got excited. I shared my thoughts about that with Victor, but he disagreed.

His room was spacious compared to the bed space in the girls' hostels. I was still looking around when he asked me to sit on the bed. We must have woken his roommate because he mumbled a "good evening" and instantly left the room with his slip-ons flapping and the edge of his loose wrapper dragging on the floor.

"Why is he leaving?"

"To give us privacy."

"Privacy for what? I thought you invited me for a poetry session?"

"Yes. Others will soon come."

He excused himself and stepped out of the room. A few minutes later, he came back with some meat pie and a bottle of Fanta. He sat next to me in bed and we ate in silence. He told me to relax on the bed and be comfortable. I told him that I was okay. He moved closer to me, and I could feel the cold edge of his arm. I wanted to spring up and run back to my hostel, especially when quite some time had passed and there was nobody else knocking at his door for poetry. He held my back and I sat still and stiff. Nkadi's voice said in my head, "How would you know unless you tried it?" I relaxed, and then he kissed me. I thought it was going to spark some feelings inside of me the way Nelo's and Star's kisses did. Nothing. The kiss lingered. He thrust his tongue deep down my throat. I cringed. I felt nothing but disgust. All the saliva that came from my mouth because I was on the verge of throwing up, I pushed into his mouth. He got up, rushed to unlock his door and then spat outside. That was my chance.

I made for the door. Headfirst, I plunged through the slight crack, widened the door and took off. I almost fell on my face but recovered quickly enough to keep darting forward. I didn't bother looking back. I scuttled straight to my hostel. After every few steps, I looked back to make sure he didn't come after me.

When I got to my room, gladly, my roommate was not there. I hurriedly locked my door and flopped on my bed. I kept telling myself that what I did was horrible. I shouldn't have listened to Nkadi's advice. I didn't like boys. I didn't like men. The kiss was never the same. I didn't feel the kind of glow I felt in the pit of my belly when Nelo kissed me. I worried about how to face Victor when I returned to the department the next day. Then I practiced the lie I would tell Nkadi about the visit. But I cringed at the thought of facing both of them. I shrugged it off, but my heart was still thumping in my chest.

I must have fallen asleep because a loud knock on my door woke me up in a panic as I tried to wipe the sweat on my face with my hand. My pillow was drenched. The room was rather hot even with the windows open. Another knock. It was louder this time. I didn't want to be disturbed. I didn't move so that my squeaky bed would not betray me. My mind ran to different directions wondering who it might be. Then Ng called out, "Unomaaaaa!" Without saying a word, I flew out of my bed and flung the door wide open and ran into her arms.

"Where were you?"

"Sorry, I had to go home. My mother was sick and my father sent for me."

"You didn't even leave a note or a message or anything."

"I told my roommate to tell you. She didn't?"

"No. But come inside, let me lock the door."

"Why?" she asked with a frown.

I was torn between telling her that I really liked her more than a friend, and that I wanted something more than a friendship, and letting her know what happened to me in Victor's room. I was arguing with myself in my head. If I told her I liked girls, it might make her accept me as something more than a friend. But I worried about rejection. I didn't want to shock her.

While she stared at me still expecting an answer for why I wanted the door locked, I decided to tell her about Victor and what happened in his room. I told her that my friend tried to get me a boyfriend by hooking me up with a random guy in our department, and the boy invited me to his room and kissed me. To my surprise, she laughed and asked why I went to the boy's room alone, that I should have gone with a friend so that the guy wouldn't try to do anything I didn't want. I told her that the issue was not even with going there alone, that I just didn't find guys attractive. The smile disappeared from her face. I hesitated before I continued by telling her that it was because I wanted to make sure that I didn't like boys and that was why I went to visit Victor. She insisted she didn't understand what I was trying to say. Then I told her that I really liked her and wanted to be more than her friend. This time she chuckled but there was a tinge of nervousness in the inflection of her laughter. Then she asked me the dreaded question.

"Are you a lesbian?"

"No. Yes. No. Does it matter?"

"It may matter because if you want me to be more than your friend, that means you want to relate to me the way a man would relate to me, so that makes you a lesbian. Instead of a man, you want a woman."

I felt rejected. I couldn't look at her again. She told me about lesbians in her secondary school, but she was never a part of that group. I felt a cloud of shame hover over me. I found myself apologizing to her. She said there was no need to apologize but that if I wanted a family, a husband and children, I should change my ways. I was still staring at my toes as she spoke. I asked her if she would still be my friend. She laughed again and held my chin up, asking me to look at her. There was a brief moment of confusion because I liked the feel of her hand on my chin. Why was she being affectionate? I still couldn't look at her though. With a hug, she told me it was okay. We'd remain friends. She told me to pray about it and that she would pray for me too. "There is nothing God cannot do," she concluded. She then clapped her hands in a dramatic way and said that we shouldn't be indoors when "Ofala," the traditional festival organized by students, was abuzz behind Balewa Hall.

In the open field between the school cafeteria and Balewa Hall was a throng of people dancing and screaming in excitement. As we got closer, we could hear quick-paced traditional music and saw a couple of masqueraders twisting in a circular dance move. High and low voices mingled as friends shouted in greeting while slapping each other on shoulders and some on their behinds. Flutes and thumps of drums and metal gongs rent the air. There was a traditional dance group from Nkpokiti, a town known for its skillful dance. Massive masquerades clad with raffia leaves hopped about. It was cultural week, as Ng told me, and Ofala day. Students celebrated the day as it would be done in a traditional village setting. A female student was crowned the queen, while a male student was crowned the king. I did imagine a scenario where a queen and a queen would be crowned as royalties of the day, and I knew that was delusional of me, but for a few hours, I forgot my worries and moved to the rhythm of the beats. I needed to see the crowned queen and king, but the crowd was huddled tight. I pushed my way through and gradually moved forward to get a good look at them.

The queen was a smashing light-skinned and average-sized lady. Her sensuous lips pouted and the thick, red lipstick accentuated her oval face. I asked the person standing next to me if she knew her name. It was Nneka. I wanted to ask if she knew her hostel and her department, but I didn't want to embarrass myself, so I moved to a different crowd and asked another lady. I didn't want to ask a guy. From my experience, they would usually go from answering questions to becoming interrogators themselves. Ladies always kept it short and straight to the point. The lady I asked told me that Nneka stayed in Slessor Hostel and was in the theater art department. I made a mental note of it and tucked it away for future reference. I had to look for her.

At the end of the festival, I couldn't find Ng. We had lost each other in the crowd. The sun was hanging glow but had a fierce beam that didn't let me see faces well enough. Shading my eyes with my left hand, I scanned the thinning crowd, saw her at a corner talking to a guy and walked to her. She introduced the guy as her classmate, and he invited us to the suya spot near Eyo-ita Hostel. Digging my teeth into a chunk of well-spiced meat was a good way to end the evening. Eagerly, I followed them to the spot. He was quite generous. Each of us got a generous wrap of suya in oiled newspaper sheets. As I munched on my meat, I observed that Ng was giggling rather too much and the guy had his hands all over her, from her shoulders to her hands to brushing against her thigh sometimes. I excused myself and said something about needing to run to my hostel before I peed on myself. Ng asked me to wait for her, but I insisted that I couldn't. The warm feel of the suya in my hand was comforting as I rushed back alone.

The next day, I had to be up early to study for a test at our departmental library. I always found it cozy, and the books were magical companions. It was at the library that one of my classmates announced that our grades for Modern Theater were out and I needed to check mine. Most people failed, but there was no way I could have failed it. Theater and history were some of my favorite classes. I was shocked to find out that I had gotten a C in the class. I had to find the professor so he could explain the grade.

I rushed off to Professor Nkwo's office. His door was closed. I decided to knock. He responded and asked me to come inside. As soon as I stepped in, he grabbed me. I was taken aback. I didn't know him well enough. Besides our few exchanges of "good morning" and "good afternoon," I didn't know the man from anywhere. I pulled away and ran to the end of his office. He followed me until I was forced to run around and around his office table. He seemed to be enjoying the chase and kept at it. I watched him closely, trying to duck his every lunge, and then paused for a moment to think.

It felt surreal. It was as if I had walked into a den of evil spirits. How did I end up in such a situation between being told grades were out and a few minutes' walk to his office? This man was always stern and well-spoken in class. I respected him. The only thing I found odd about him was his tendency to grab his bulge in the middle of a lecture.

Before I could completely finish my thoughts about my predicament, he lunged at me again. I dodged too hard and knocked some of the books on his shelf to the floor. A voice called out from the hallway, "Is everything all right?"

My mouth was open to scream, but no sound came out because he had interjected with, "Yes. Everything is fine. I am just trying to kill a rat."

"Do you need help?" the voice asked.

"No! I got it. I am okay."

I closed my mouth and gazed at him. He had to be playing a prank. Maybe he was just a comical character that never showed that side of himself in class.

Out of the blue, he apologized and said he was just being playful, expressing the same thing I had thought. He asked me to sit and offered me some nuts and orange juice. I politely turned down his offer and told him I'd come to find out what I did wrong in my test. He waved his hand at me and told me not to worry about it. It was a trial test, he said, and went on to explain that he was working on some research and needed some students to assist him for extra credit. He asked if I was interested. I said I wasn't. He said I should think about it, but that I could come with him to the main library in town to look for some books. "We won't be long," he said.

He gathered some notebooks and asked me to grab some of the pens on the basket near his side table. We'd need the pens for notes. Then we entered his stuttering red Beetle car. Its exhaust pipe erupted with blasts of black smoke. Even as the smoke trailed us, he zoomed off as if trying to speed away from it. The explosions from the exhaust pipe died behind us. The black smoke faded into the air. As he drove, he didn't speak, but there was a strange smirk on his face.

About an hour later, he stopped in front of a huge green gate and honked. A lean man with torn shorts flung the gate open and bowed to him in greeting. The place didn't look like a library. We stepped out of the car, and the gateman had barely closed the gate behind him when he bolted ahead of us and struggled with a bunch of keys as he tried to open a door for us. I didn't realize where we were until Professor Nkwo shut the door behind us. It was a hotel.

I ran back to the door, forcefully pulling the doorknob. The door wouldn't open. He calmly peeled off his clothes until he was stark naked. I didn't know where I got the courage from, but I glared at him, and especially at his erect penis with its patch of bushy hair. I was shaking, but I had to think fast. Even if I screamed, we were no longer in his office where there was some kind of traffic. Nobody was going to rescue me. He seemed determined to have sex with me. It was either that or he would hurt me and rape me. I decided to play along. Luckily, I was on my period. Perhaps, he was one of the men who didn't like having sex with women on their period, and I had used a rag because I could rarely afford sanitary pads.

His erection was turgid. He thrust it between my thighs with my skirt on. I told him that I would love to have sex with him, but that I was on my period. He said it was okay, he didn't mind blood. He wanted to start by rubbing his penis around my vagina. I told him that my flow was heavy. He ignored me and squeezed my left breast as he massaged his penis. I didn't know what came over me, but I pulled off my skirt and then gradually unwrapped the menstrual rag from my pelvic region. The stench of stale blood overtook the room and hung thickly over us. He instantly sat up, holding his nose, and asked me to dress. By then, his penis had shrunk.

He drove back quietly to the campus. My grade was changed to a B the next day. I avoided him like a plague, and he never bothered me after that incident, but the anguish of the experience lingered for a while. It felt as if I were avoiding everybody including Ng. Every so often, she would check in to see how I was doing. My attraction to her waned with time because the guy she had introduced to me as her classmate eventually became her boyfriend.

20. Wind Gusts

I KEPT TO MYSELF until my department started planning a literary event that would include mock newscasting. I was one of the students assigned to gather news items from different students and different departments. I was excited about both gathering pieces of news and being a mock newscaster. It also became a good opportunity for me to seek out Nneka.

When I got to her department, I asked one of the students if they knew her. The student led me into another room with a stage and pointed at her. She was on stage acting. The sight of her took my breath away. My eyes were glued to her every movement. She was in love with a guy her age, but her father wanted her to marry a rich older man. So she plotted an escape with her lover. They were caught and separated. I could be her lover, and we wouldn't be caught and separated. My mind rewrote the script. The stage lighting gave the scene an allure that transported me to another world, a world where she was my queen and I was her queen. We would be in bed with feathers and scented candles, lost in each other's arms, swimming in the songs of our love. My heart rate increased. I had to stop myself. Instinctively, I looked around. Somebody might be reading my mind and rat me out.

At the end of the play, there was rambunctious applause and a standing ovation. A number of people went backstage to commend the actors. Apparently, they knew the actors. I was not sure about what to do. I sat there waiting and wondering, hoping that she'd step into view. When most people had gone and the actors and producers were packing up their costumes and clearing the stage, I saw her walk toward the exit door with her hands full of clothes. I galloped up to her and helped her gather the edge of her cloth that was dragging on the floor. She seemed startled. I introduced myself and told her that I was at her coronation during the Ofala festival and I just wanted to see if I could make an appointment with her to interview her about the coronation for my departmental event and news articles.

She didn't seem to be a very friendly person because there was a stubborn scowl on her brow. She said she was too tired to talk but that I could meet her in her room on a Saturday or a Sunday at one p.m. I jumped up with a jubilant "yes!" That was when a smile crept up her face. Her eyes were like a pair of golden ponds. Beautiful. They reminded me of Nelo's eyes. She asked me my name even though I had mentioned it to her a couple of times. I didn't mind. I gave her my name again and even proceeded to tell her that my grandmother gave me the name and why she gave me the name. She sighed and gazed at her fellow actors, who were drinking palm wine at the other end of the theater. I stopped talking. She walked toward them, yelling a "see you then!" at me. That was enough for me, except that I had hoped to hug her or at least touch her hands.

My thoughts lingered on her eyes, and I remembered Nelo again, this time with a pang of guilt. I felt as if I were cheating on her. But I was restless. I didn't want a convent to be the only place I could be with the person I loved. I had suggested we run away to a big city. She had laughed at the idea of the two of us running away to a place where nobody would recognize us so we could live together. Agreeing to her suggestion was not off the list of our possibilities, but the foundation of that idea was still shaky to me. I was feeling as if I was going to lose her. Maybe I had already lost her. Even though anxiety was gathering in my mind, I was looking forward to seeing Nneka.

Outside, the temperature was warm, the residue of a fierce sunny day. However, the cool winds rolling off the surrounding hills seemed to have merged with the dissipating heat. I hadn't quite walked a few steps away from the theater department when I saw a shadow teeter toward me.

"Hey!"

I heard a faint voice and was somewhat afraid. For some reason, I entertained the notion of being attacked. I clenched my fist to steady my nerves.

"Sorry," she said. The shadow became a girl. "Are you going to the hostel?"

I said yes. Then she asked if she could walk with me. I agreed. She was lean and tall. The glow of the moon teased her smooth caramel complexion. She was quite pretty too. She asked if she could go with me to my hostel. There was another rehearsal for her in a few hours and she didn't want to go all the way home and then head back for the rehearsal. I didn't mind at all, and I told her. Her face widened with a smile. I asked for her name.

"Nnenna," she said. Then she added her last name, and I clapped my hands in excitement. Her father was our music director when we performed *The Mikado* at Queens Nsukka. I instantly hugged her and every bit of shyness fell away. I kept telling her how wonderful her father was, he was a god of music, and she chuckled with the praise I gave him. We chitchatted about theater and music as we approached my hostel.

From a distance, the hostels seemed to be engulfed by darkness. The harsh, piercing lights radiating out of the windows gave some life to our surroundings. Closer, we could hear blasts of the latest disco songs. A few feet away from my hostel, the music grew louder. Reverberating sounds of different songs drowned the chatter of girls standing around Okpara Hall. A variety of cars zoomed in and out with beaming headlights and screeching tires. In a corner, a group of drunk boys were engaged in a shouting brawl. I couldn't help but snicker when I overheard an exchange between the group of boys and an acquaintance passing by.

"Oh, boy, going to see your babe?"

"Yes, oh. Wetin man go do again."

"Lucky you, man. Nothing for us. We dey here dey roast."

"Ah fit get one babe for you as you desperate reach."

"You be idiot! Useless man! You fit die for woman. Meanwhile, you dey starve. You chop once a day: carry over oh-one-oh. Dey chop okpa, carry garri soak am becos you wan maintain woman. Big fool! Your papa go hear about your mumu ways."

"May your tongue be blistered. Bastard!"

"Na you go born bastard with dat ashewo wey you dey carry. Useless idiot!" His voice boomed into the night with every explosive hurl of idiot he flung on the passing guy. Eventually, he ignored them and walked on. Drunk men had a vicious quality. They painted the picture of a boiling tank of detonating testosterone. With a stifled simper, I hurried on, so glad to be far away from them. Nnenna increased her gait to catch up with me. Before I stepped on the stairway of Okpara Hall, I took one last glance at another isolated corner of my hostel where a couple clung to each other and were ferociously kissing. Why couldn't I have the same freedom to kiss my lady just like that in the open, in public? I questioned the unfairness of it all, but kept walking.

In my room, I asked Nnenna if she wanted something to drink. I couldn't afford much, but I had some canned milk and Lipton tea. She agreed to a cup and told me how kind I was to have warmly welcomed her into my space when I was just meeting her for the first time. I told her that as soon as she told me she was O' Ndu's daughter, she became my family. She laughed and tilted her head to the side. There was a kind of performance in her every move. Her personality swayed with grace and class, and it was topped up with her smashing beauty. Her gestures were heightened with a dashing smile and pair of sparkling eyes, and her near-hoarse voice caressed every fragile edge of my reality. Her mind was like a deep ocean. She knew something about everything. Our conversation felt to me as if we were making love: stimulating and engaging. I think I may have gotten slightly wet as we carried on talking. Beautiful, intelligent women can keep me talking until time dissolves around me. The end to our conversation felt like somebody snatched me out of a magical dream: my roommate asked us to lower our voices because she wanted to sleep.

That night, as I escorted Nnenna back to her department for her last rehearsal of the night, I had the urge to ask her if she liked women or if she was only into men. A voice in my head told me to calm down and take things one step at a time. Perhaps it was the deprivation I felt that made it easy for me to find almost every pretty woman attractive. Maybe it was just my hormones raging. Maybe they raged twice as hard because of some love deficiency. I was laughing to myself, and she asked me why. I told her that I was just thinking out loud. I really wanted to tell her everything about me, to lay myself bare because I found her fascinating and wanted to be able to be myself around her. I found her self-effacing and brilliant flair attractive.

I stayed and watched her rehearse. She took on a different personality on stage. It was amazing that she could transform easily and become the character she depicted. I was further taken in. When she asked if she could sleep in my room after the rehearsal, eagerly I said yes. My bed was small, but we managed well. The next morning, I asked her if she wanted some "Bambara nut" cake, "okpa," and some tea. We ate. That was my regular breakfast. It was not just cheap, it was filling too.

We talked all morning and into the early afternoon. We were engrossed in belly-bursting laughter about some lecturer who had the habit of having sex with students on top of his office table and he forgot to lock his door. One day, a cleaner had walked in on him and his sex buddy. Instead of the cleaner getting hysterical and running off, the lecturer was the one that got into a frantic rant and bolted out of his office with his pants halfway down his legs. We were still bellowing when a loud knock stopped us in our tracks.

It was Nelo's sister. I called her Adanna. She came to tell me that Nelo was arriving in a couple of days to see us. "She is really coming to see you. I bet she used me as an excuse to get my parents' approval," she said with no emotion on her face. She followed up with "Who is your friend?" looking at Nnenna.

I introduced them even though Adanna seemed not to have the patience to let me finish the introduction when she grabbed the knob of my door to announce her departure. I asked to accompany her to the main hostel door, but she refused and waved a frantic goodbye.

The door slammed, and I found myself arranging all the items on my table. When I was done with arranging my desk, I continued with my closet. I placed loose clothes in their proper places and straightened out crooked-looking ones. Nnenna was amused. "Is Nelo coming to inspect your room?" We both burst out laughing.

"Don't mind me," I said.

"Why? Are you nervous?"

"No. Not really."

"That Adanna doesn't seem too nice. I hope Nelo is better. I guess not, because you are already putting things in their proper places."

"You are wicked!" I yelled at her, and we laughed harder.

It was a Saturday, and that was the day I was supposed to meet up with Nneka. I decided to ask Nnenna about Nneka. Her revelations about Nneka were not so encouraging. Nneka was from a wealthy and renowned family, so she tended to be snobbish and had a no-nonsense attitude toward life. I was almost discouraged from keeping the appointment. She insisted that her assessment could be wrong and that I should go.

At Slessor Hall, Nneka was not in her room. Her roommate merely grunted an "I don't know" and never took her eyes from the book she was reading. I walked out and remained in the vicinity. Thirty minutes later, I saw Nneka emerge from a silver baby Benz. She was decked in an all-white suit and glittered like a gem under the rays of the sun. I gaped, too afraid to say a word, and hoped she'd recognize me. I could feel the glare of her eyes through the shade of her horn-shaped sunglasses.

She strapped her brown leather bag over her shoulder and faced me. "Unoma, right!"

I was so happy. My heart jumped. I found myself skidding toward her. She stepped back. I could feel the confusion on her face as if she was surprised at my reaction and was not sure if I wanted to run into her or hug her. When I stopped right in front of her, she stepped back some more to put space between us. The vanilla scent of her cologne teased my nose and left the taste of cotton candy on my tongue.

"I'm sorry I'm late. I had to go to town for a meeting," she said and briskly walked toward her hostel. I followed closely.

She entered her room, let me in and then locked the door. Surprisingly, her roommate was not there. Then she started ripping off her clothes and exclaiming about how unbelievably hot the weather was. My eyes shot straight to her supple breasts as they flopped out of her white brassiere. Her curvy body looked like well-carved wood; it was tantalizing like an aesthetically pleasing work of art.

I gasped under my breath and swallowed hard. Whatever beautiful image I saw was too far away, and I was reaching for what I couldn't have. Because I didn't want her to see the lust in my eyes, I pinned my gaze to the portrait on her wall. I heard her sink on her bed and clear her throat before I looked her way again. She had changed to a loose, large T-shirt. Her thighs were lithe with a touch of luminescence. Every move she made was like a dance. She asked me to take a cold drink from her mini refrigerator close to her closet and give her an apple juice. I had never seen such an array of assorted drinks and beverages in any student's refrigerator in the history of my stay in that school.

"What do you want to ask me?"

"Ehheerrr…" I found myself stuttering.

"Something about coronation?" she reminded me.

My questions were vague. I asked her what interested her about the replication of traditional ceremonies and titles in school. She told me that because she was crowned the queen of her hostel, just like the male hostels came up with their own crowned kings, they decided to celebrate it further to give it a sense of traditional royalty. Within a few minutes, I ran out of questions. She stared at me. That made me uncomfortable, but not until I realized that she was not actually looking at me. She had a habit of zoning out. After a long awkward silence, I told her I was ready to leave. She asked me to take as many beverages as I wanted. Then she shifted her weight, face down on her bed and grabbed her pillow. My eyes took a quick sweep of her legs, and then persisted along her calves. So much saliva gathered in my mouth that I incessantly swallowed. I wished I could transfigure myself and become her pillow, even for a few seconds.

Drowsily, she asked me to press down the knob of her door to lock it when I stepped out. I took one last glance at her and gently shut the door. Under my breath, I cursed myself. I should have asked her if it was okay to drop by and say hi or to come to her department to watch her rehearse. I should have told her that I made a new friend in her department who rehearsed at the same time as her. I should have told her that I would be back with more questions. I should have told her that I wanted to be her friend.

I kept muttering to myself until I got to my room. I needed to masturbate. My roommate was there, and the toilet was too repulsive. It reeked of stale shit and was littered with maggots and chunks of dried feces. I couldn't use it. I wanted to run out into the open fields and scream until I passed out. I was so randy I could have stuffed any woman's fingers or tongue up my vagina. I had to control myself.

21. Rain Showers

Nelo's visit quelled my desperation for other women. Between my room and her sister's room, we were often chastised for always locking the door or for being too affectionate toward each other. My roommate told us to stop the way we behaved because it freaked her out. We had no privacy. Her sister's roommate developed a habit of glaring at us, until one day she asked us if we "fingered" each other. Nelo turned near red in rage.

"I don't appreciate you saying that," she stammered as she addressed Obiageli, her sister's roommate.

"Then stop acting as if you are boyfriend and girlfriend! Stop acting as if you are lovers. If you don't lock the door, you are in each other's faces giggling and grabbing each other! Stop it!"

"So that means we are fingering?" Nelo asked with another stutter. This time, her eyes were half closed, and she was shaking with rage. I could see her long eyelashes clump up.

At that point, I wanted to gather her in my arms and kiss and make passionate love to her. Instead, I gnashed my teeth and joined her in telling Obiageli that her accusations were vile. I had to make sure my voice was not loud because that would be seen as disrespectful since she was older than us. I held Nelo's hand and led her out of the room.

We took a long walk from Slessor Hall down to the school mail room, through CEC and then down the patches of weed-covered footpaths. The path between the stadium and toward the only mosque UNN had was isolated, so I clutched her lean waist and nestled my face in her neck. She laughed and said it tickled and pushed me away. I was so happy to hear her laugh. The image of birds twittering in lush trees on a bright, sun-soaked day came to my mind. I held her again and whispered into her ear that she was the most beautiful goddess in human form I had ever beheld. She laughed again.

"So you have seen other goddesses in human form, but not as beautiful, right?" she asked, looking straight into my eyes.

"Emmm, yes. No. What I mean is that—"

"Yes, like Nnenna, your new friend," she cut me off before I could finish and slapped me hard on my buttocks. "You and your candy mouth!"

"Wait. How do you know about her?"

"I have my ways," she said with a frown.

I wanted to grab her again but noticed a group of male students behind us. We stayed quiet and waited until they had passed. Whenever she was angry, all she needed was a few minutes to cool off and she would be back to her old self again. It was either she was left alone to cool off or she would take it out on the person who wouldn't give her the time and space to deal with the anger. I had been her victim, so I knew better.

We kept walking past the mosque toward Franco and then stumbled into Obukpa Road to Zik's Flats. Nelo kept a straight face and walked with a determined comportment. Her strides were always firm like she was on a catwalk. Each sway thrust her forward as if pushing against a stubborn wind. It was one of the many things I loved about her.

Close to Zik's Flats, there were some restaurants and stores. We scanned some of the makeshift restaurants, trying to figure out which of them had the fewest people. There was one with a couple engrossed in conversation. We walked past them and sat at the rear corner of the restaurant. The lady in charge, a plump, middle-aged woman, hurried to us to ask what we wanted to eat. We asked for two bottles of Fanta and one meat pie. She told us that she had just finished making hot pots of okra, egusi, and ora soups with goat meat. We insisted on the drinks and meat pie.

Nelo's company was always a joy. The school of optometry where she was on a two-year program while she waited for an admission into medical school was on a two-week break, so she had decided to take a week or more off to see me and then spend some time with her sister. As we sipped on our drinks and munched our meat pie, there were always things to laugh and giggle about.

We hadn't quite made it halfway with our drinks and meat pie when two men strolled into the restaurant. One of them yelled, "Fine girls! How una dey?" Nelo looked at him as if he were not speaking to us. I didn't respond either or bother looking at him. He came closer and asked if we didn't hear him. I politely responded that we were doing well and thanked him. He asked why we shared one piece of meat pie. I told him that we were not hungry. He faced Nelo and asked why a beautiful lady like her hardly spoke. "You can't be this beautiful and mute at the same time," he said and laughed. His friend laughed too. His friend had ordered two bowls of egusi soup with goat meat with eba or pounded yam.

"I am not mute," Nelo finally spoke up.

"Of course! You are too beautiful to be mute. What is your name?"

"Mandy," Nelo lied.

"What is your name?" he asked me.

"Felicia," I said.

Nelo kicked me under the table, and I almost betrayed our secret when I laughed but then made it seem like a cough. He introduced himself as Henry. His friend waved at us and said, "Emeka, here."

A young girl of about sixteen hurried out with two steaming bowls of egusi soup and placed them on the table for us. We looked at each other, our mouths agape.

Nelo shook her head. "I don't want this," she said to Henry. "Thank you."

"It's okay. If you ladies are ready to go, they can put the food in takeaway containers for you."

We looked at each other and then got up almost at the same time. They insisted we stayed to chat with them, but Nelo was not having it. She even rejected their food and briskly walked out. I hurried after her.

"At least, give me your room numbers!" Emeka pleaded with us.

When I caught up with her, I suggested that we try another restaurant. She refused. Then I suggested that we go and sit at what was called "Lovers' Garden" near CEC. That was where we ended up. I told her that we would have gotten a free meal and that I was really hungry. She said that she would rather starve than eat a meal bought with those bastards' money. I was used to being interrogated and asked for my hostel name and room number. She said that people seemed to be more respectful at her school.

Eventually, we got around to the talk about getting into the same convent and staying possibly at Enugu or in the east. I knew Nelo deeply wanted to dedicate herself to a religious life. I was spiritual too and wouldn't mind doing the same, but the terms had to be different. She was more sincere than I was. It was, perhaps, her calling. She was pure at heart. Kind in thoughts and deeds. However, I felt as if I were beginning to fade in the picture she tried to share with me. I wanted her, and a convent might provide a roof for us. She wanted God and me to share the same roof. That was how I read it.

We did look at possibilities of convents. We had the option of our mother convent, Holy Rosary. There were others: Divine Love Daughters, Handmaids, Immaculate Heart, Dominican Sisters, and Sisters of Notre Dame. I promised her that we'd start the process again when I graduated from the university.

For the rest of her stay, our days were filled with snatching whatever time alone we could get in my room or her sister's room, taking long walks, lots of laughter, plans, and dreams. Nnenna had conveniently stayed away. On the day Nelo returned to her school, we both cried and clung to each other as if our lives depended on it. We didn't care about prying eyes or the questions about why we were so emotional. We hung on to each other until she was forced to pull away in tears. I accompanied her to the Nsukka Park with her sister and then waved a frantic goodbye when the bus took off.

Her departure brought me back to the same feeling I'd had on the first day I landed at UNN: forlorn, stripped, and vulnerable. But Nnenna was still there for me as a loyal friend. My cousin too, Buchi, had taken a break from England and had just enrolled at UNN. There were things to look forward to, except that without Nelo, life seemed incomplete.

With time, I settled back into my routine. Nelo and I exchanged letters to reassure ourselves and to stay up to date with events at school. Our world seemed small and confined. There was no place to run. We barely found spaces to talk and look deep enough into the pain that bound us. We bore a love that was too heavy for our small frames. Every step we trod with that love threatened to hurl us down; it was too weighty for us. I pondered. I wondered why this love that could never express itself was to be borne or made to exist. What was the use? Why make us prisoners even before we had a chance for trial?

These were some of the questions Buchi tried to help me find answers to. She assured me that my love for Nelo or any other women I fell in love with was legitimate and that love had a right to live. She told me not to mourn what hadn't died and doesn't die. There was hope for me yet. I held her words close.

She was one of the few lights in the tunnels I traversed in search of answers and in search of the right to be. Often, I felt unworthy, and all that people saw when they tried to peek into my soul was a woman unworthy, clad in rags of sin and abominable stench. Often, I wished I could pour all my stench into a bottle and cork it so that its foul smell wouldn't escape and betray me. Often, I gathered my rags around me to stop them from flailing in the wind; a shameful sight. My incessant apologies for my offensive existence wouldn't do. Glares and angry scowls chased me deeper into a suffocating hole.

While Nelo and I existed under the cloud of doubt that stayed with us, we tried to live while we waited. I met more women I found attractive, but they were like Ng and Nkadi: I had to try harder with men. Another man, and another man. So, I pushed Nelo to the side and tried a relationship with another guy. This time, I liked Zaachi. He was smart and handsome. If it was about finding out if I enjoyed sex with men, then I had to try. I hadn't had sex with a man. I didn't know if I could still be redeemed.

Everything was okay between me and Zaachi. Literature, poetry, writing, and the theater were the highlights of our talks until he invited me to his room one day. When he touched me, I recoiled. I had to remind myself that I was trying to get comfortable with who I was. I had to have an open mind and relax to receive any transformation that was to happen. I stayed calm. Again, I reminded myself of my mission: I needed to know if I could have sex with a man. So when he kissed me, I bore it. When he tried to thrust his penis into my vagina, I bore it the way I bore the agonizing push of a constipated shit. I had to know for sure that I didn't like sex with men. His penis wouldn't and couldn't penetrate me.

"Are you a virgin?" he asked. I said yes. He seemed upset. Hastily, he picked up his underwear from the floor and pulled on his trousers. After looking at him for a few seconds, I pulled my skirt back on. There was a long silence. What could be wrong with any girl being a virgin? I thought men were glad to take away women's virginity, to be able to brag about being the first. I left his room.

The next guy I dated was a tall, slim, and handsome Hausa-Fulani man: Sabo. I met him at an event in the mass communication department. I liked him instantly because he spoke crisp Queen's English and his skin had an irresistible dark glow. I was surprised that Nkadi was not happy when I announced to her that I was dating a Hausa-Fulani man. Her concern was that he might be keeping a harem of women in Kano as his wives. I was not bothered. Marriage was not my goal. I had to see about this sex thing with a man. And Sabo was particularly nice and tolerable because he was not adventurous in bed. He didn't start with caresses and kisses, playing with my breasts and then finally working his way through to the real act like most Igbo guys I dated did, all of which I found very irritating. Sabo knew how to do it: mount and hump away. He was the one who finally took my virginity when I was twenty-five. And he was the one who made me understand that having sex with men was not for me. I gave it up.

Buchi was there to tell me again that if men were not my thing, I should let it go. I posed questions to her that even God might not be able to answer. She kept saying that the answers would come with time. I was in her room one day, waiting for her to come back from her classes, when a tall, alluring lady knocked and walked into the room. I barely looked up when she walked in. I was flipping through Buchi's novels. I told her that there was nobody in the room. She laughed a hearty laugh and asked if I was not somebody. I smiled, blinked several times as I beheld her radiance. She smiled with a dimple, and her skin was flaxen like a caramel plum. She sat down not too far from me on the bed without asking. She said that she needed to catch her breath and was actually looking for Buchi's roommate, who was in her study group. Then she introduced herself as Maureen.

I really found her attractive, so I took the bold step of offering her one of Buchi's Coca-Colas. I knew she would kill me, but Maureen looked thirsty. She refused it and I asked if I had water instead. I asked her to tell me about herself. She was in the botany department because she loved plants. She was from Onitsha and had more brothers than sisters. As soon as I heard the word, Onitsha, I leaped up and told her that she could be my sister. Onitsha was not far from Asaba. She laughed and hugged me and said I was adorable. It was foreign to me. Nobody had ever hugged or held me and told me I was adorable, except for Nelo. The warmth of her hug tingled down my spine. I liked the feeling. She left a note for Buchi's roommate.

When she was ready to leave, I asked her if it was okay for me to escort her to her room so I could visit her when I had the time. She accepted. Her room reminded me of Nneka's room. It was well furnished, and a sherry fragrance hung in the air. If we had not entered Bello Hall, I would have sworn that her room was not in a UNN hostel. Her album was the first thing she grabbed to show me. Then she asked me what I wanted to drink before opening her refrigerator. With a can of orange juice and a glass, she sat next to me and gave me the juice.

"Let me pour it for you," she said.

I gulped down the juice and almost choked. It was her closeness and that tingling feeling. Then she gently rubbed my back and asked if I was all right. She did not stop caressing me until I stopped coughing. I was tempted to keep coughing. Her touch felt good though I was a bit confused. Nobody was quite as tactile as Maureen.

When I returned to Buchi's room, I couldn't wait to tell her about Maureen. She didn't seem as excited as I was.

"She's obviously older than you. Maybe she was just playing the role of a big sister."

"It can't be. There was some seduction going on," I said loudly.

"So? You think there is something there?" she asked and smiled. "You are always running away with your imagination. Don't get your hopes up yet. Visit her a couple of times and we can see where this takes you."

"Don't jinx it for me."

"I won't. But from what you've said, she does not sound like a regular girl. So she is bisexual, a lesbian, or just a nice woman. Whichever, don't get your hopes up."

I wanted to be as realistic as Buchi, but Maureen was special. I hung on to the hope that she'd turn out to be more than a friend. Buchi encouraged me not to visit her the next day, to wait it out. Give it a few more days, she had said. That sounded too long, so after a couple of days, I visited her. She seemed happy to see me and gave me a lingering hug. I wished Buchi could have seen that. But, when she announced that she was running late for fellowship, I paused. "Oh shit!" I muttered under my breath. I prayed that she was not one of those born-again girls. If she was, it was surprising that all that time I spent with her, she never tried to preach to me.

Within minutes, we were headed to Abiding Word fellowship. Their venue was quite close to the school cafeteria, not far from Balewa Hall and my own hostel. At the other edge where the venue of the fellowship center nestled were Isa Kaita and Akpabio, male hostels just at the edge of the road that led to the university medical center. I heard the band playing a couple of blocks away before we got there.

There were a few people there when we arrived. There was a masculine-looking girl standing next to a slim, dark-skinned girl who was fiddling with a microphone. She would croon into the mic and then tap it for volume. The masculine-looking girl took the mic from her and tried to adjust it by wrapping her hand around the mouth of the mic and twisting the rings around it. As she wound the edge of the mic, she folded her lips and intermittently licked them. I blinked several times in disbelief. How could this gay girl be on this campus and I never met or stumbled upon her? I couldn't believe it. She was clearly a lesbian like me. What could she be doing here? I waved at her and she clearly saw me, but she ignored me, nodded and continued with the mic. I was still scratching my head when Maureen ushered me to a chair.

As soon as Maureen excused herself to say hello to a handsome guy she had called "Brother Chidi," I walked up to the girl and introduced myself, and she gave me a knowing smile. Her name was Ona. I boldly told her that I was looking forward to fellowshipping as well as making more friends. She nodded again. Then I asked her if it was okay to get her room number and be friends with her. She didn't hesitate. Her hostel was right next to mine: Balewa. I was feeling disconcerted. Maureen turning out to be a born-again Christian and bumping into Ona was a bit too much for me. I was cringing within myself. Nothing ever worked out the way I wanted or planned it. I bet Buchi would say that she had warned me not to be too eager. I did, however, decide to make the best of the situation.

In no time, the place was buzzing with life as Pastor Mike emphasized every word of Jeremiah 20:17. "I will restore you to faith and heal your wounds, declares the Lord…" he said out loud as he clenched his teeth with every completed sentence. Each verse was punctuated with an "Amen!" Meanwhile, I was looking around, admiring the many gorgeous girls in attendance. I couldn't believe that there could be one gathering with so many stunning girls. As difficult as it was, I tried not to get distracted. As Pastor Mike read, something about the book of Jeremiah touched me. I had so many wounds. Would I truly be restored to faith and would my wounds be healed?

I was enjoying the song. One Sister Kate sang Yolanda Adams' "Through the Storm" as Brother Nnamdi pounded away at the piano. I became nervous. The tidings of the fellowship seem to strike a chord in me. Adams' lyrics appealed to my agony. The storms in my life were blowing. Would they go as they come? I wouldn't say that I had been calm and doing fine when they met me. Was Christ the captain of my ship? Would I ride through the storm? I was hesitant, nevertheless, about buying into the lure of a spiritual rapture and a spiritual healing. I have often suspected every born-again Christian as an agent of hate trying to attack me.

Everything was going well until it was time for altar call. Those who had not given their lives to Christ were asked to surrender to God. They were to walk up to the makeshift altar near the pulpit. I was determined not to go. Maureen touched me. Her touches were often soft and sweet, but this time there was a spark near electrical in it. She whispered in my ear that she'd go up with me. I felt a mixture of anger and betrayal. How would she know if I had already given my life to Christ? Why would she make that assumption? I got even more nervous. I had always felt that when it came to binding and casting, pastors found me worthy. They were the insects and I was their nectar.

It was praise and worship time. People started speaking in tongues as Pastor Mike laid hands. I made a conscious effort to stay far away from him at the edge of the line where we all stood. He made for me though, and slammed his hands on my forehead. I took a few steps back and looked behind me to make sure there were no chairs I could trip over. I stayed calm as he prayed. I was not sure if he was expecting something to fly out of me before he ended the prayers. He was relentless. I figured that if I started dancing or fell to the ground that the ordeal would end. I danced a slow dance. The push didn't stop. I increased the vigor of the dance. Nothing. Then I fell, and he invited all the assistant pastors, including Maureen, to pray over me. I didn't know until then that she was one of the pastor's assistants. He asked Sister Kate to follow up on me and make sure I was okay and attended fellowship regularly. Maureen interrupted and said she was already working with me.

After the fellowship, I couldn't wait to bolt out. It was another hope dashed. Maureen wouldn't let me go. She sensed that I was agitated and asked that we talk. We got to her room, and she apologized for making me go to the altar since I didn't seem to want to go. I told her it was okay, and that I wanted to be honest with her. I told her I was a lesbian and found her really attractive. Surprisingly, she was calm. She said it was all right with her, but that she preferred men. I was happy she took it in good faith. However, she shared some bible passages with me. When evening came around, she invited me to go and pray with her at the lawn tennis court near the school stadium.

First, we sat down at one of the benches there and talked about my sexuality. She told me that she wouldn't judge me but wanted to know if I was willing to fight it. I told her that I was not sure about what to do because there was nothing to fight. We went back and forth until the shrill sounds of crickets interrupted our conversations. We stood up and she held my hands and asked me to open my mouth and pray to the Lord for salvation and redemption. It felt so fake to me. I could be quiet and still pray for whatever.

We were in the middle of the prayers when a troop of men gradually emerged from the surrounding darkness and encircled us. I wanted to run but she held me tight and asked me to concentrate on the prayers. She screamed out louder as she called the name of Jesus. Just as they surrounded us, they disentangled and dissolved into the night. Maureen and I waited for a little while before we made our way back to her hostel. We had just escaped the wrath of cult boys. Unknowingly, we had walked into their meeting spot.

***

After the whole fellowship and cult boys' incident, I only saw Maureen occasionally. She didn't stop looking for me though. If I was not in my room when she came looking for me, she would leave me notes and addressed me as "darling," "love of my life," or "sweetheart." I wondered why any woman would refer to another woman, a lesbian at that, who had professed her love for her, as darling. If that was not meanness of some sort, I didn't know what was. Of course, Buchi was always there to analyze things to clear my infantile muddled head. She would say that people could still love me but not sexually. She would tease me and say that it was equivalent to agape love as we say in our fellowship. We'd laugh as I confessed to her that I'd rather have carnal love than the agape one. I remained friends with Maureen and even visited her at Onitsha during one of our school breaks. Just like Ng though, she too faded into the background of my life.

I did visit Ona in her room. At first, she was somewhat standoffish, but because I was eager to confirm my suspicions that she was a lesbian like me, I didn't let her being snobbish stop me. She was indeed a lesbian, and she was in the fellowship for the same reason I was there. There was a girl she really liked. The girl led her to Abiding Word and she had been trying to abide ever since. We weren't close, but we remained friends. I wouldn't have used her strategy for going after girls she liked, but I did see her reason. Most of the most beautiful girls on campus seemed to be concentrated at Abiding Word fellowship.

Though I did go back because I loved the music and the beautiful women, those reasons ended up not being strong enough to sustain my interest. There was a lot I thought was superficial. Sounding and singing like African American gospel artists was impressive by itself and somewhat entertaining to me, but I needed something deeper and genuine to make me stay. There were times in the past when I actually called myself a born-again Christian and was a member of the Scripture Union. I was a member of an evangelical group. That phase didn't last because it felt as if I was doing it out of compulsion and the censuring that came with it didn't help: no elaborate earrings, no trousers, not even a dab of lip gloss was accepted. I left and wondered why I joined them in the first place. At that time though, it was the trend. Everybody was "Born Again" and something was wrong with those who did not profess to being so.

On some nights, I cursed myself for being a homosexual. The nights the pastors prayed over me and hammered Paul's words to the Romans 1:26, 27 in my head:

> Because of this, God gave them over to shameful lusts. Even their women exchanged natural sexual relations for unnatural ones. In the same way the men also abandoned natural relations with women and were inflamed with lust for one another. Men committed shameful acts with other men, and received in themselves the due penalty for their error.

I failed to ask why verse 25 was often omitted:

> They exchanged the truth about God for a lie, and worshiped and served created things rather than the Creator—who is forever praised. Amen.

This verse seemed to focus on idolatry and of rites that perhaps happened during idol worship involving vulgar activities as part of the worship. This idea was far from standing side by side with a loving, same-sex relationship.

Then my questing would often end with the Book of Romans chapter 2:1:

> You, therefore, have no excuse, you who pass judgment on someone else, for at whatever point you judge another, you are condemning yourself...

In the five-day deliverance sessions with Pastor Mike of the Scripture Union, I was closely studying the bible myself. The five-day prayer session was to cure me. When I got tired of being dragged around like a common criminal, I claimed healing, but I left Scripture Union. Maureen brought me close to this experience again. Ona seemed to live the life as a cover-up for whatever deeper meaning and desires we all want.

22. Dusts and Dirt Paths

THE SCHOOL BREAK arrived. It was a relief. I needed a break from the dry Nsukka air. I wanted to spend more time with my cousin Buchi. I wanted to see my mother too, but ultimately, I wanted more time to sleep and ponder on why a union between me and Nelo seemed to be fading with every passing day. I pondered on why I couldn't find any other like me to form a friendship or a relationship. Ona was the closest I could get to any of my kind. She seemed ashamed to be associated with me, or was it that she was self-conscious? Perhaps she didn't want to compete with me for women. Or maybe she hated me for existing just as she existed. We both had to feed our hunger with whatever foods of desires we could scrounge up for meals.

Asaba had the same chill in the air just like the Nsukka air, but it was December so the harmattan was encroaching. My days at home were mostly quiet. Occasionally, I chitchatted with my mother; our conversations became rowdy and tense when she cooked beans too many times in a week. Whenever she did that, I knew she had no money. To appease me, she would ask me to eat it with some garri soaked with sugar.

I was on the floor one day, close to her feet when she asked me, "Unoma, do you have a boyfriend yet? You are almost graduating, so it is okay now to have a boyfriend."

The last spoonful of beans I was eating almost choked me. I scrambled for the cup of water beside me, took a couple of gulps before I found my voice.

"I have not found any man I like yet."

"Okay. This is a good time to be warm and friendly. Don't reject men because of their looks. Some may not look as handsome as you like, but their character is what matters. Okay?"

"Yes, Mama. But, can I join the convent to become a reverend sister?"

"No. We are not Catholics. Just because you attended a convent school and lived with reverend sisters does not mean you should become one of them."

"Mama, you are Anglican, but I converted and became a Catholic."

"Are you going to argue with me, or are you going to shut up?"

I hurried off the floor and cleared my plates. I went into my room and turned on the radio to listen to one of my favorite radio hosts from FM Enugu: Golibe. Many a night I masturbated to her voice. It was sensual, husky, and soothing. I always imagined that she was speaking exclusively to me. Steamily subdued by Golibe's voice, I dozed off.

There was water surrounding me, and this woman...I couldn't quite see her face, but I recognized her: large breasts and long dreadlocks. The dream was too vivid. I told my mother about it. She was silent for a while. She finally spoke because I didn't stop staring at her, waiting for any interpretations or what she thought about the dream. Finally, she said that the woman in my dream was Onishe, the river goddess.

"Why do I keep seeing her?"

"Just pay attention. Maybe she is trying to tell you something." There was so much concealed in silence.

"Is that a good or bad sign?"

"She is a mother and a spirit. She is not a bad being."

I knew that she was not a bad presence because my grandmother always invoked her to protect her and her children. But why would she want to send me a sign? I looked at my mother again. Worry was gathering around her face. She grabbed her hymnal and hummed away. I went into my room to write Nelo a letter and then to write in my diary. I had planned to write until nighttime came upon me, but a sharp pain jabbed at my groin area and seemed to have rippled down my legs to my feet. I knew the pain. My period. I dreaded my period the way I'd dread being sliced into pieces with a machete. The pain always felt as if a zillion fire ants had invaded my uterus and ate away at me with an intense bloodthirst. The urge to dig my hands into my belly and yank off this beast implanted in me would overwhelm me. My uterus felt like a foreign body sent to torment me. I had no use for it. I didn't want it. Then my wailings would start.

My mother knew the routine. She would give me some painkillers, a cup of scorching tea, and some hot water to gently massage my belly. When none of those helped, she would run around the neighborhood looking for overripe watermelon, slice it into two and let me stare at the peeking black seeds of the watermelon. It was something I couldn't explain. Watching the seeds was like watching whatever ate into me. The red-fleshed watermelon was my uterus. Watching calmed the pain.

I got too comfortable and forgot the hot cup of water on my belly. The water tilted and landed on my thigh. I screamed and flung everything around me into the air. My mother came running in. My notebooks and my diary got wet. My mother gathered them and tried wiping the dripping water from them. She used the edge of her wrapper. Then she took them outside to dry in the sun. I was doubled over in pain. I must have fallen asleep. When I woke up, she was standing over me. I panicked. I had never seen her like that before. She sat down.

"Who is Nelo?"

She had read my diary.

"You want to escape to the convent with her? Is that why you don't have a boyfriend?"

"No, Mama. That is just a story I made up." The frown on her face got deeper. She didn't believe me.

"This had better be a made-up story," she said and rushed out. I had a bad feeling that settled at the pit of my stomach where the demonic cramp lodged. I was not sure about what she was going to do. I wished she would beat me up or do something to get it over with.

Five days later, when my period ended, she asked me to dress up because we needed to see somebody. I kept asking her who we were going to see. She didn't say. I dressed up and followed her like a sheep headed to a slaughterhouse. We ended up at Pastor Nwite's church: the Cherubim Ministries. There, Nwite, the pastor with glazed eyes and clumps of tangled hair, announced that we were to start a seven-day deliverance session. He looked crazy to me.

I looked around. My mother had disappeared. At the far end of the large compound that contained Nwite's church was a beautiful woman, maybe in her early twenties. She was nursing a baby. Beside her, the flames of her fire flagged in the air. There was a gentle breeze. I gauged the fence of the compound because I wanted to get away from there even if it meant jumping his fence.

I had to wonder. What made my mother trust this man to leave me here with him for prayers and deliverance. He said we were to start that night. This was after he had admonished me for refusing to cut all ties with what he called water spirits. I didn't want to believe that he knew what he was talking about, especially after I had discussed Onishe with my mother. Or did she tell him something?

That night, he asked me to kneel. We were in a shallow room at the opposite end of his church. He had called it his holy sanctuary. There was an altar draped with long red and white cloths. Candles were numerous, from red to yellow to white to black and blue. As he faced me, he started a familiar prayer and I almost hissed under my breath.

"Get out of her you wicked gods of the sea! Vamos!"

"Gods of the sea?" I wondered. "Another fool," I muttered.

Then he grabbed a humongous bell and rang it over my head repeatedly. The sound threatened to give me a headache. Doggedly, he clanged away. I closed my eyes and tried to shut out all the noise, until he abruptly stopped and asked me to lie down. I hesitated for a few minutes.

"I won't harm you, but I must exorcise the evil spirits from you."

I lay down, and he sprinkled some ashes on my forehead. Then he turned around and snatched a thick, black, leather-covered bible from his cloth draped-altar, pulled open a page with a worn bookmarker and started repeating these words:

If they do not change their ways, God will sharpen his sword. He bends his bow and makes it ready; he takes up his deadly weapons and aims his burning arrows.

He kept repeating these words and it started to sound like a chant that was about to put me in a trance. He stopped abruptly. I was to come back the next day, the same time.

I came back the next day. It was the same thing for the next five days. On the sixth day, he said we had to go down to the river to sever the final ropes binding me to the spirits of the river. At first, I was anxious. Flashes of my drowning incident overwhelmed me. I closed my eyes and took deep breaths. I didn't want to drown. We walked deep into the river, the water came up to my breasts. He left me there and waded his way up to dry land. From the spot he stood, he yelled what I should expect.

"I will keep praying from over here. You will eventually see Mammy Water. She will show her face. Don't be afraid to look into her eyes. Tell her that you have denounced her. Tell her that she does not own you. She will try to touch you. Don't be afraid. Don't run. My prayers will cover you. She will not be able to touch you as much as she tries."

I was shivering. He was raving like a mad man. I didn't believe his dumb words. The water was getting chilly. I wanted to sail out of the river and tell the man to go to hell. But I wanted to complete this process to redeem myself and to prove to my mother that there was nothing wrong with me. If I didn't complete the seven days of prayers and deliverance, my mother might say that I was not willing to try and be saved.

I stood there in the middle of the river as the waves pushed me back and forth. In near panic, so many thoughts clashed in my head. What if a hippopotamus sprang out of the blue and attacked me? River snakes. But the waves ebbed, and a calm wind seemed to have eased the flow of the river. I stood firmer and thought about my mother, my grandmother, and Onishe. They could protect me. I could feel the clay sands giving way under my feet. I would feel like I was sinking and then I would be steadied.

I waited to see Mammy Water. There was nothing. Even the rustling sounds of the shrubs where Nwite sat became silent. I was counting the minutes and the hours. It felt like eternity. I turned around and saw a shadow scrambling away, tearing through stunted shrubs as if being chased. Another long silence. Then a whiff of marijuana assailed my nose. I started shaking violently from the cold. There was dead silence, except for the washing of the waves and the sounds of wild owls hooting from afar.

I rocked my way to the dry land and then scuttled through the bushes in the direction I thought we came. The large, tall leaves of elephant grasses slashed away at my face as I frantically surged forward trying to retrace my way home. Dim lights ahead helped me follow a path that looked familiar. I heard voices and hurried toward them. Two fishermen were disentangling their fishing nets under a streetlight. But as soon as I lurched toward them, they froze. Then they abandoned their nets and galloped into the night. One of them almost fell. He steadied his frame and kept sprinting. I wanted to ask them for directions.

Finally home, I opened the door without knocking. My mother was sitting on the couch reading her bible. I broke down and started crying. I told her that Pastor Nwite left me in the river and took off without saying a word. She was not angry. If she was, she didn't show it. Patting my back, she asked me to calm down and to change my clothes before I caught a cold. Even after I narrated every detail of the sessions, she only apologized and insisted that I had to return the next day to complete the seven days of prayers. She was going to be with me this time, she said.

At Nwite's church, we met the young lady. This time, she was peeling cassava tubers. She greeted my mother and gave me a long stare before spitting. She told my mother that Nwite was in his prayer room and pointed at the same place where he conducted his deliverance sessions with me. He must have heard my mother because he came out to meet us. He promised my mother that he would bring me home safely and that she didn't have to wait for me. Even with my cry of protest, he persisted. The young lady grunted at us and quickly assembled her peeled cassava tubers into a basket, hurled it upon her head and scampered into one of the rooms attached to the church.

The prayer session for that day was different. He had rearranged all his prayer items to another corner of the room. Even his draped altar was moved to the corner of the room. I was aching to ask him why he abandoned me at the river, and why he ran. He offered me a chair and sat down a few feet away, facing me. He kept looking down. Then he asked me.

"You didn't see the people in the water?"

"What people?" I asked him, baffled at his surprise.

"Their sight didn't scare you?"

I felt so irritated at myself, my mother and at the stupid man who called himself a pastor and a man of God. He was either delusional from the marijuana he took or he was mentally unstable. He wouldn't stop asking me. I almost yelled at him to complete the session and let me go home. As he prepared his altar with candles and incense, he kept casting a mixture of anxious and furtive glances at me.

I studied the room more closely. There were strange pots at two corners of the room. There was only one window to the right of where I sat. One side of the window had a loose bolt. On the floor close to the window was a mattress. It was there the last time I was there, and I figured it was where he slept on nights of long prayer. This time, though, the mattress was neatly covered with a blue bed sheet and two pillows instead of one. There was only one pillow when I'd seen it the previous day.

When he finally finished arranging his altar, he told me to remove my clothes and lie down on the mattress. I instantly sat up and refused.

"What kind of prayer requires that I remove my clothes and lie down?"

"Your vagina has been locked. I need to anoint it with oil and then break the chains in them."

I had to think fast. His main door was already bolted. I was too dumbfounded to say anything more to him. I watched his every step, especially when he walked up to his altar for the third time, muttered something to himself and made the sign of the cross. Then he swung around and faced me. It was then I saw the bulge protruding through the long green gown he wore. As I stared at him, tears started running down my cheeks. He told me not to cry, that he would use oil and be gentle. When he turned to get the jar of oil on his altar, I took one last look at his wooden window and threw my whole weight on it and smashed my way to the other side. With all the pain crashing through my body, I scrambled up in a flash. I scaled the fence a few feet away from his window. I kept running until I got home.

Out of breath, I met my mother and my younger brother at home. I fell at my mother's feet, crying uncontrollably. "Mama, he almost raped me! He is a fake pastor! He almost raped me!"

My brother held me and asked me what the problem was. He kept asking me who hurt me. I looked to my mother to say something. Instead, she told me to lower my voice and calm down. My brother started yelling at her to tell him what was going on. I told him that the pastor our mother took me to for prayers almost raped me. All he heard was "rape," and he lost it. He dragged me with him to show him the pastor. My mother kept yelling at him not to embarrass her by stirring the curiosity of the whole neighborhood, that it was something we could peacefully address. We ignored her. We ran down the road as I led him to Pastor Nwite's church.

On arrival, I pointed at the gate of Nwite's church. My brother kicked it open. The young lady was standing by the side of the gate with a bawling baby in her arms. She was still gaping at us with the shock of our forced entrance. My brother asked her about Pastor Nwite. She told us he was not home, that he had hastened away a few minutes ago and didn't say where he was going. Curious, she asked us what the problem was, and I told her about the prayer session and how Nwite almost raped me.

She laughed. I was surprised by her laugh.

"What is funny?" I asked, almost tempted to slap her. She strapped her baby to her back and offered us chairs to sit down.

Her parents had attended Nwite's church until he prophesied to them that she was possessed by the marine spirits and needed deliverance. It was during the seven-day prayer deliverance that Pastor Nwite got her pregnant. Her parents abandoned her with him.

"So that was what he wanted to do to my sister too? To rape her the way he raped you?" my brother bawled at her. "Where is his church?"

She pointed in the direction of his altar. My brother scattered all the candles and jars of oil on the table and flung the table upside down. He almost set the altar on fire, but I told him that there was no need. The young lady pleaded with him as she wriggled the matchsticks out of his hand.

"Tell him to leave this town today and never return because if I meet him here when I come back later today, he will be carried to where he came from as a corpse!"

The lady nodded at him as she pranced back and forth trying to pacify her wailing baby. The commotion had woken him up.

23. Droughts

In the weeks that followed, my mother was full of apology. As much as I forgave her, I couldn't get rid of the sick feeling I had about the ordeal. I contracted malaria. The medication I was taking made me hallucinate. The whole experience with Pastor Nwite haunted my dreams. I asked my mother if she believed that I was under the spell of water spirits.

"If you are under any spell of any water spirit, it is not a bad spell. I just want you to marry the man of your dreams, have children like every other woman and be happy."

I would look at her even more confused, but I couldn't confront her with the secret my grandmother divulged to me. She always kept things to herself. When my father died, she wouldn't confront his demise; there was no discussing it. We spoke about it in hushed voices so as not to upset her. She wouldn't confront my brother's restlessness about people constantly calling him a bastard because he couldn't say where his father was from. The only words I knew of my father's family was Nwan Ukan. She had told me that when she took me home to see my father's parents that my paternal grandmother hurled me in the air with pride and kept saying *Wan Ukan*. When I asked her what Wan Ukan meant, she said it meant child of Ukan. Ukan was my father's village in Benue.

I became more withdrawn. When things occurred to me, I asked her. I asked her if she knew the bible verse that Pastor

Nwite recited. I remembered it so well because it bounced around and tormented me for a long time:

> *God is a righteous judge and always condemns the wicked. If they do not change their ways, God will sharpen his sword. He bends his bow and makes it ready; he takes up his deadly weapons and aims his burning arrows. See how wicked people think up evil; they plan trouble and practice deception. But in the traps they set for others, they themselves get caught. So they are punished by their own evil and are hurt by their own violence.*

With her bible, she flipped through some pages and announced, "Psalm 7: 11 to 16." I took her bible and read the whole of Psalm chapter 7. I was shaking. Some things seemed too coincidental to be true. The same Psalm from verse 1 to 8 said:

> *O Lord, my God, I come to you for protection; rescue me and save me from all who pursue me, or else like a lion they will carry me off where no one can save me, and there they will tear me to pieces. O Lord, my God, if I have wronged anyone, if I have betrayed a friend or without cause done violence to my enemy – if I have done any of these things, then let my enemies pursue me and catch me, let them cut me down and kill me and leave me lifeless on the ground! Rise in your anger, O Lord! Stand up against the fury of my enemies; rouse yourself and help me! Justice is what you demand, so bring together all the peoples around you, and rule over them from above. You are the judge of all people. Judge in my favor, O Lord; you know that I am innocent.*

I clung to it as I pushed through two weeks of malaria bouts after the experience with Pastor Nwite. In that time, my mother nursed me with extra care. She refused to leave my side. I didn't know if it was out of guilt or remorse. She became more loving than combative. Within a couple of days of my recovery, I wanted to talk. I had to see my cousin Buchi.

The long walk to her house at Ezennei helped me to get some air and clear my head, though the intermittent honking of cars made it a bit uncomfortable. I had walked through Ogboogonogo market, right through my grandmother's place. I had not quite made it past Abu-ato primary school when a young girl of about eight bumped into me with a tray of ice water on her head. She muttered an apology and hurried on to a bus. The driver of the bus had waved at her. He wanted ice water.

That scene reminded me of the days I sold ice water too. It was during one of the periods my mother left us, this time with my aunt, Nkeonyeasua. She had four kids of her own plus me and my younger brother. Altogether, we were six kids in the household, and she had to find ways to make ends meet. Besides the ice water business, she also had a beverage and provision store right in front of my grandfather Nsugbe's compound.

Those days of selling ice water were stressful and were made even more stressful by the motor park touts who would pinch my buttocks and dare me to do anything. Or those who made me chase after them to pay when they snatched one of my ice water bottles. Many a day I had lost money because when they snatched the bottles and ran into isolated places in the market, I would be too afraid to follow them any further. Giving up on chasing after them, I prepared myself for a beating when I got home because my aunt, my mother's older sister, always thought I was too careless. I was making her lose money.

One incident when I had followed the thugs too far, two of them grabbed my breasts and squeezed hard until I cried out.

It was a driver who came to my rescue. The large basin of ice water on my head tilted until it almost fell as I struggled to pull my breasts away from them. I had developed large breasts by the time I was almost nine. Always embarrassed by their size, I wore thick cardigans even under the heat of a scorching sun.

Buchi was cooking rice and stew when I got to her house. The short staircase at the back door of her kitchen was often my favorite place to sit whenever she was cooking. I sipped the Sprite and munched on the cookies she offered me and shared my worries with her, especially that I had "outed" myself to my mother when she read through my diary. But she thought it was a good thing that my mother found out because she would learn to accept me as I was.

I didn't agree with her. I thought it was more complicated than that. She would always look for ways to cure me. I didn't think she had given up even with Pastor Nwite's vile incident. Besides that, I was also bothered that my mother had been quiet about my father's family in Benue state. She didn't want to tell us the exact village and town my father's parents were from. She may have been afraid that we would have wanted to return to them. Maybe she was afraid of losing us to them. Her discovery that I was a lesbian made it worse because the not knowing my paternal family was another level of rejection for me.

"But you know that has nothing to do with you. It's your mother's problem and maybe she is protecting you," Buchi said.

"She can't be protecting me and my brother when she already told me that they don't want us."

"Again, it is not your fault. You were not consulted before they decided to birth you, just as you were not consulted about your sexuality before you realized that you are homosexual. Don't be too hard on yourself. None of these issues have anything to do with you. Not your fault."

I tried to explain to her that the pain came full circle for me: being treated as less at the hands of relatives, or so I felt, being rejected by my father's family, and then this, my sexuality.

"Sorry if I am repeating myself, but all these are their issues. Nothing to do with you. You are a beautiful, smart, and promising young lady. And you will grow to your full potential. Focus on that, not the pain, not the past, and not on people's judgment of you."

I was quiet for a while before Buchi walked into the kitchen and I could hear a clatter of plates. As we ate in silence, I watched the sunset through the largest window in her living room. The weakening sun reflected a haze spread across the evening sky. Then I hurried with eating, but Buchi said to take my time, that she would give me a bus fare back home. So we prattled on about life, about love, and about returning to school late into the evening.

***

School at UNN started, and our routine resumed. My major challenge that semester was computer science. It reminded me of math. The formulas and the equations never made sense to me. This time, I was taking a computer science class that was supposed to be practiced with a computer, but there were no computers. Instead, we were crammed into a large auditorium in the engineering building to listen to a computer science lecturer yell and draw diagrams on a board. I had no idea what he was talking about. I failed the class twice. In my three years at UNN, it was the one class I kept failing. I had to pass it as a requirement to graduate.

I was on my way to meet another student, Chidi, whom my roommate recommended to help me study computer science before the next exam when I saw a distinct crowd milling around in front of the general studies (GS) building right next to my department. I got close to some of them and listened. They were Americans. Then I walked up to a couple of them, two ladies, and asked them if there was a special event going on. It was the Women in Africa and the Diaspora (WAAD) Conference 1992. The venue was the GS building. Excited, I thanked them. I had to attend this gathering. I bet there would be poetry and story sessions at the conference. I had to be there, but I hurried on to meet Chidi for our computer science appointment.

With little to no idea about what the conference was about, I eagerly gathered some of my poems and a couple of short stories and headed to the GS building. At the entrance were some ladies seated at three tables while some wrote their names on assigned papers. I hesitated and watched, wondering if I was supposed to write my name as well. Ahead at a corner close to where the three tables were set was the sign: Registration. I shuffled back. I was not invited. Then I snuck past small crowds and entered the main auditorium. The back door of the auditorium led directly into the theater-like hall. That was where I entered and then looked down at the stage. There was a petite woman, dressed in all white with long dreadlocks.

A fierce sense of déjà vu engulfed me, and I could feel cold shivers spread across my body. The hall was not cold but I was shuddering, yet I couldn't pull my eyes away from her. She was reading. There was something intensely familiar about her, but she was an American, an African-American. I could tell from her accent. As I listened to her read, stronger pangs of familiarity flooded my psyche. An intense, bizarre feeling overwhelmed me. I got scared. I couldn't explain what was happening, so I sat on the closest empty chair I could find to steady myself. It had a broken arm.

I looked at her again. This time, our eyes locked for a few seconds. She must have smiled, I think. I knew this woman. I had to think. I was deeply drawn to her; it was a fiery feeling. I rested my back on the chair to be more comfortable and waited to see when she finished reading and where she sat. With a standing ovation, she walked off the stage and sat a few places away from it. I couldn't go and talk to her without blocking people's views or distracting the next reader. I waited.

A few minutes later, she made her way up to talk to some people. I hurried to her but stopped her midway. She had one of the most disarming smiles I had ever seen. She introduced herself as Leslye Huff. Her presence was soothing. Then it came back to me: Onishe's frame flashed across my mind. It couldn't be. They were the same size: enormous breasts, long dreadlocks, dark glowing skin. She kept smiling at me as if she could read my mind. I introduced myself to her. Her stare was piercing, so I looked away often. She asked that we sit. Then she tugged at my hand and asked me what I had crumpled up. I had crushed my poems and stories after I'd heard some of the attendees read their poems. She insisted on seeing them, or maybe I willingly showed her the poems. She liked them. Suddenly, I blurted out that I was a lesbian. Perhaps, I was trying to explain the message in the poem. She chuckled.

"I am a lesbian too."

I think I became almost mute after she said that. Were the pieces of the puzzle that was my life beginning to take form? From that moment, I didn't leave her side. I followed her to her hotel room, but she refused to let me sleep in her room. She was in a committed relationship with Amina Mary. I was crushed. Her friend and next-door neighbor at Ikenga Hotel was the only alternative option for a place to lay my head for the night. It was late for me to head back to campus. I stuck close to her and accompanied her everywhere she visited at Nsukka until she returned to the US. When she left, I was heartbroken. I told everybody I wanted to know about her: Buchi, Nelo, and even my cousins. Before she left, she gave me all her contacts and promised to reach out to me as often as she could.

Time for graduation grew closer. My plans with Nelo, always in the background, became glaring. I had to give the convent a shot, though I was not sure if Nelo had agreed to wait until I finished the National Youth Service Corp, which every Nigerian graduate was required to enroll in for one year, or if we would go ahead and apply to the same convents during my Youth Service. The so-called compulsory one year of service to my country seemed like a waste of time, but it gave me the opportunity to think seriously about living a religious life and finding my paternal family.

For Youth Service, I was posted to the northwestern region of Nigeria. It used to be part of former Kwara state. During my two-week camp for Youth Service, I visited one of the convents at Okene to see if I would apply. I told Nelo that I didn't like the town. It was mostly perched on rocky hills. Because the area was close to Benue, my father's state, coupled with the fact that other graduates who were also at the NYSC camp were from around Nigeria, I decided to use that opportunity to ask if any Youth Corpers were Tivs, my father's ethnicity. There was a handful of them. Incidentally, one of them knew my father's family from a village called Ukan in Ushongo local government. He also knew my father's story. I was overtaken by joy. I begged him to take me there. He did.

The night we arrived at my grandfather's compound, there was a stillness that felt like ice. Then a stooping, thin, older man stepped out of the low door of his thatched hut. There was a cluster of huts around his. Then what seemed to be a clatter of voices trooped out of the other huts to greet me. It were as if my dead father had resurrected. My grandparents clutched me as if I were about to bolt. They said they didn't abandon us, that my uncle, Ayila, exploited their vulnerability and scammed them out of thousands of naira with the promise to find us but never did.

They said they were poor farmers with little money, barely able to survive. They said they were hesitant about an Igbo daughter-in-law but started loving her as soon as they heard she had borne children for them. They asked that I forgive them.

Eventually, I took my brother, Ugonna, to meet them. Because they had moved to Zaki-ibiam, their new farm settlement, there were no cars to access their location. So we took cars, boats, and bicycles until there was nothing else to convey us. We walked twenty miles and eventually arrived. My brother became calm after the visit. He realized that he was not a bastard. He had a father and he had a family. I, on my part, had my closure.

Back at my station at the National Service grounds, I ended up applying to another convent in the same region but asked for a trial period where I could come in and spend some days to see how they lived and then make up my mind. It was not planned, but I got into a relationship with the mother superior. It was a loving and genuine connection. We spent tons of time together, traversed the diocese and cities across the Benue River and beyond. We wined and dined at high tables, and I tasted the luxury of the reverent life. Bishops' mansions. Servants. Huge kitchens. Resourceful cooks. Well fed. Content and swaddled in the soft cotton sheets on some of the nights, we soaked ourselves in the lavender-laced fragrance of the pillows. Restless, though cushioned in that cozy cot, wrapped in each other's arms, The Fugees' "Killing Me Softly" serenaded our slumber.

The parts of our trips that became drudgery were the long prayers and masses. In convents, I couldn't focus. My eyes always found a way to settle on the rounded rumps of sisters. With every salacious glimpse, I whispered a prayer. But our trips abruptly stopped when we were involved in a car wreck. Her driver hadn't checked the car for maintenance, and on one trip, the brakes locked and plunged us into a ditch right next to a river. Shattered window glass lashed us across the face. There was only minor bleeding, but that incident halted our travels.

Inasmuch as I enjoyed the relationship, it left me flustered. I was no longer sure I wanted to become and remain a nun. I didn't want to have sex with women in the shadows of a church. I hadn't gathered the courage to let Nelo know, but when I confessed my unfaithfulness to her, she flew into a rage and cut me off without words. The next thing I knew, she was so livid that she enrolled in a monastery where she would neither have a social life nor see me as often as I wanted. At least, that was how I interpreted it.

After one year of compulsory service to my country as a graduate, I headed home to Asaba. My mother was happy with me for a successful completion of university. However, she was still eager to see me with a man. A couple of months into my stay at home, she practically kicked me out. "Go and marry or find a job!" she said. The next day, I found myself in Lagos on a friend's invitation.

24. Lagos: Shorelines

LAGOS WAS SHOCKING at first sight. When I stopped at the Ojota motor park as my friend who had invited me to Lagos directed me, I was afraid to step out of the bus I had taken from Asaba to Lagos. The throng I saw through the window was the kind of crowd I had never anticipated. I heard myself muttering "Jesus!" The driver of the bus yelled at me to get out. It was his final destination.

Ojota was a crescendo of noises and people milling. It was as if there were a competition for who could yell the loudest. Honking cars and buses were not left out of the chaos. Then teenage girls and boys cried out the names of their wares for anyone who cared to buy. "Buy banana!" "Buy oranges!" "Mineral!" "Gala!" All these rang out in the thick Lagos air. As I stood, still trying to take in the haste of the environment, a middle-aged woman shouted at me to get out of her way. "Are you lost?" she yelled.

It was then I gathered myself and remembered what my Lagos friend told me to do: *When you get to Ojota, look for a big bus, a molue. The ones that will be calling out Ojuelegba.* There were buses moving in opposite directions. I was not sure which side to be on for the Ojuelegba bus. The size of the molue and the way people hung on its doors almost gave me a panic attack. How was I supposed to mount such a bus and shove my way through the mass of bodies hanging like dangling fruit in a wild wind? As I cautiously stepped away from a mound of human excreta, my heart palpitated at the thought of asking any of these swift humans any question. Their quick gaits didn't seem to encourage delays or questions.

I plucked up the courage and walked up to a tall, dark-skinned, shirtless man. He was sprinkling oil over the meat he was grilling and squinting his eyes from the smoke of his smoldering charcoal. I waited and then he pointed to the other side of the road. Overhead was a bridge, which I was thankful for because I wouldn't have known how to race across the busy road. The bridge was littered with floating plastic bags, beggars with decaying eyes and ears, hawkers straightening out the clothes and shoes they had displayed. I cringed at every smell, sound, and sight, and clutched tighter to my sizable traveling bag, which was strapped across my shoulder. As I descended the stairs of the overhead bridge on the other side, there was yet another crowd of hawkers aggressively plying their wares.

I stood with a group of people who seemed to be waiting for buses. I watched them race after the bus and swing themselves in. I kept biting my lower lip. What if I fell and landed in one of the pools of muddy water? My immediate worry, though, was that I hadn't yet heard any bus or molue call out Ojuelegba. All I kept hearing them bellow was "Elegba! Elegba!"

I must have stood there for hours waiting for the right bus. Evening was fast approaching. The sight of wheelbarrow pushers hustling to ferry people's bags and luggage to different nearby car parks and a few fights breaking out behind me didn't help my racing heart. I had to ask somebody about how I could get to Ojuelegba. I eyed the lady selling shoes under the pedestrian bridge. She was fanning away flies as she sucked on an overripe mango. Even though her eyes were bloodshot and the veins on her arms were bulging, she seemed to have a calm disposition. I inched closer to her, estimating the right time to ask her the question. When I got close enough to ask her, I almost stammered. "Aunty, abeg where ah go see Ojuelegba bus?"

"You deaf? See all these buses na Ojuelegba bus!' she shouted and took a powerful swing at a fat fly heading straight for her juicy mango.

"But dem dey say 'Elegba,'" I replied nervously.

She let out a throaty laugh as a thick mango pulp slid down her hand. She lifted her hand and caught it with her stretched-out tongue before it could drop to the ground. I was surprised when she sat up and walked up to me and said, "Elegba na the short name for Ojuelegba." She looked down the stretch of the busy Ikorodu Road and then told me to be patient, that she would help me get into a molue. It was cheaper. A few minutes later, another molue lurched its way toward us. She called out to the conductor hanging on the door handle. "Akpan! Abeg help my sister enter!"

Akpan hopped down as the molue kept moving forward. He was straightening out a wad of naira notes he had and motioned at me to move faster. I held my swinging bag close to my chest and took off after Akpan. By the time he lifted me with his left hand and shoved me into the hot, overcrowded bus, I was out of breath. I craned my neck to see if I could wave a thank-you to the shoe seller, but the windows were blocked by people's heads.

My ordeal started when I got to Ojuelegba. I walked around the whole overcrowded motor park, just like Ojota if not worse. When I asked questions, I was either ignored or glared at. I bought an orange from a woman and used the opportunity to ask her where I could get a bus to Aguda market. The buses heading to Aguda were flanked to her right.

I was relieved to eventually arrive at my friend's house. There was food and a chilled bottle of Sprite waiting for me. Her younger sister Oma and parents were there to welcome me as well. They laughed at my Elegba story and said it was usually the case for first-time travelers. I got comfortable with them, and my Lagos friend started referring me to places I could find jobs. I dropped my resume at each of the companies. After a couple of weeks,

I started getting closer to her younger sister. She was quite friendly and funny, pretty too. My stay with them didn't last. I was kicked out of the house because I was accused of getting abnormally cozy with Oma.

Oma snuck out of the house to escort me to the house of one of my schoolmates from UNN. Nkadi was happy to see me and informed me that her father had been looking for a fresh English graduate who was passionate about writing to take a tour of the country and collect folklore from different parts of Nigeria. She had recommended me but was not sure about how to reach me. It was like a dream come true. There I was, fresh to Lagos, no employment, and already homeless. Nkadi's father offered his place for me to stay. He also offered me a position to be the coordinator of a book club he was going to start when I got back from my folktale collection tour.

Within six months, I was done with collecting Nigerian folk tales. It was time to edit and compile them for a book. As I edited, I tended to the lending and shelving of books at the Rubik bookstore, right next to Kilo bus stop at Ikate, Surulere. My boss also hired a cashier for the days I decided to work on the collection of folk tales and wouldn't be at the book club. My job was spiced up by Oma's visits. It was with her I enjoyed flirting the most. She was smart and sassy.

Though there was so much chemistry and sexual tension between us, we never acted on it. There were certain lines I was too afraid to cross. But I would watch her talk and get aroused. When she sang, especially Celine Dion's "Love Does Not Ask Why," my nipples hardened. Her vibrato came with an extra edge, especially when she gazed into the open skies with hands outstretched as she sang certain lyrics. I felt weak. The tease in her body language and what looked like tear-filled eyes brought me to tears.

There was also an overwhelming sense of orchestra she brought with her in that song. Each time, I would fight back the urge to grab her and run my wet lips across her nape. "Think Twice" resonated with how I felt, particularly with the boundaries I deliberately created. That resolution made me think that she was speaking to me through the song. Many a night, I listened to it with my cassette player. I imagined things safely in my mind, never to be done with her. That was how I killed the sexual tension that threatened to consume me.

Then one rainy Saturday, I was at the book club when a light-skinned girl stumbled in. She apologized for wetting the floor of the store with her rain-soaked umbrella. I told her it was okay. She stood at the glass door, staring into the pouring rain. After a few minutes, I asked her if she was waiting for somebody. She said she was looking out for a car. When there was no sign of any car, she turned around and started a conversation.

We became friendly, and she came to the store more. During one of her visits, she asked me if I had a social life because she always met me reading. I asked what she meant by a social life. She said something about having a boyfriend and going out to the beaches and restaurants. I told her I had no boyfriend since I was not interested in men. It was my territory, so I didn't see any damage being done by taking a breath and revealing myself to someone who had become somewhat of a friend. My revelation seemed to have amazed her because she kept saying, "Oh my God! You are the first bold lesbian I have met."

"You have met many?"

"Not really, but those I know never say a word about it."

I asked her if she was surprised, and she said she was not surprised about the lesbians she had met but was surprised at my boldness. I was not sure about how to feel. The next day, she had managed to find out where I lived and came unannounced. I was astonished and was even more flabbergasted when she opened her legs and bared her private part at me. She had on a cream Barbie skirt with no underwear. I threw her out of the house. She was a nice person, but I didn't find her attractive and for her to have found her actions seductive was disgusting. She later apologized and we became close friends.

With time, every weekend, I started exploring Lagos. Some members of the Rubik book club who were also interested in writing told me about the Association of Nigerian Writers, Lagos branch. The association became a refuge where I would share my poems and stories with likeminded people. I met and made new friends. A few months later, I became the assistant secretary. My duties included coordinating readings and working with different newspapers in Lagos to maintain publicity outlets for the association. Within the association, a women writers' group sprang up: Women Writers of Nigeria. I became the publicity secretary and my task doubled. As I reached out and worked with newspapers, I also searched for funding for awards and event sponsorships. It was during one of those searches for sponsorship that I walked into a bank a friend had recommended. They were very supportive of art projects, he had told me.

The lady I met at the desk directed me to their corporate affairs department. At the department, I was ignored. When I asked one of the men there who I could speak to about a project, he asked me if I had a note from an authority. I was baffled. A note from which authority? They saw the look of confusion on my face and carried on with what they were doing. I was still trying to find my voice when a thick, dashing lady of about average height strutted in. Her red lipstick was the first thing I noticed, her curvy hips, and then her near-Chinese eyes. They reminded me of Nelo's eyes. She must have wondered why I was looking lost right in the middle of their lobby. With her gaze fixed on me, she walked up to me. Her pleasant lavender perfume hung around us.

"May I help you?" she asked.

"I am supposed to be meeting the head of corporate affairs, but nobody will attend to me."

"I am the head of corporate affairs," she announced, and her stare became probing as if to assess my worth. "How can I help you?" she asked.

I became conscious of my dusty worn brown sandals and my slightly rumpled blouse. To prop up my self-esteem, I dug the fingers of my right hand into the back pocket of my jeans and pushed my chin slightly forward. "I am from the Association of Nigerian Authors. I am the secretary, and I am soliciting sponsorships and support of any kind to encourage arts and writing in the city."

"I see," she said. "You are a writer too or you just work for the association?"

"I am a writer."

"I see. Let's go to my office. I am not sure we have done that in a long time."

As we got to her door, she opened it and asked me to go in first. I thanked her and waited until she asked me to sit down. Her office was upstairs, well decorated with floral curtains, a humming air conditioner, and soft leather sofas. She asked if I wanted something to drink. I said no. I gave her one of the letters of sponsorship I had. She read it and placed it in a folder.

Then she asked me what I studied and when I graduated. I told her, and she said she'd studied English as well. She asked too many personal questions but complimented me on my "beauty and brains" as she called it. At first, I thought she wanted to know if I was a fraud using the name of the Association to get money, until she told me that I reminded her of her younger self when she had just arrived in Lagos. Jokingly, she warned me to stay away from horny men who would want to entice me with their money.

"Even with their money, they don't stand a chance," I said and laughed.

"How so?" she asked, and her smile disappeared.

I got nervous. She seemed quite friendly, but I didn't want to say anything that would upset her or make her change her mind about sponsoring my programs. "It's nothing!"

"It's okay. You can tell me anything."

When she said that, I almost scoffed at her. "There is nothing to tell, but I don't like men like that."

Surprisingly, she didn't inquire further. Relieved, I sat up. She gave me her business card and said I could call her Nelly and check back next week at the same time. Then she said her driver could drop me at CMS, where I could take a taxi to my destination. She handed me an envelope and led me downstairs. Inside her car, I couldn't help but think that there was a stealthy connection between us. I became restless. Next week seemed too far to know if there was a possibility of sponsorship and to also get to the bottom of the furtive feeling I had.

Three days later, the chairman of the ANA association asked me to meet him in his office. He had heard from the bank confirming that they had received our application for sponsorship. He was surprised that I didn't show any excitement. Instead, I looked into the distance. He asked me if all was well. All was well. He congratulated me for a job well done. I nodded at him and walked off. Nelly was on my mind. I was not sure about whether to wait until the next week to return to her office or if that was the end of our transaction. Though I wanted to visit her again under the pretext of thanking her, I decided to wait it out.

A day before my return to her office, I polished my brown sandals, ironed my brown shirt with a V-neck, and wore a new pair of tight, black jeans I bought at Yaba market, the used clothes stall. Knowing that I was prone to sweating under the Lagos heat, I used some of my savings to buy a scented roll-on. When I got to her office, I was told she'd stepped out, but they didn't know when she was going to return.

I was agitated. I must have sat there in the lobby for almost two hours when her driver hurried in and told me that she'd asked him to bring me to their other office. Instead of an office, he took me to a comfy bar. I met her at a corner of the bar on a couch. She tapped her hand beside her and asked me to sit. We hadn't started talking when she downed two shots of Hendrick's gin. She asked me what I wanted to drink. I asked for malt. She laughed and asked if I didn't take hard liquor. When I told her that I hadn't really tried it, she told me that it would not hurt to try it. I could mix it with my malt, she recommended.

I nursed the bowl of goat meat pepper soup she bought for me and chewed with caution. I didn't want the soup to drop on my blouse or seem like a glutton to her. I felt a tinge of flightiness in my head. I poured more malt into my drink to dilute the effect of the gin. She sat back on the couch, demure. I sat back too, to level up her contemplation, and chewed the piece of meat in my mouth. The half-eaten bowl of goat meat was on the table beside me. I finally looked at her.

With dimmed eyes, or it must have been the dim-lit bar that made her eyes look closed, she said, "I like you a lot and I want you to be my pet."

I almost choked on the last lump of goat meat in my mouth. She didn't move an inch or ask if I was okay. I coughed.

"I am serious," she said.

My head was spinning at the unexpected way she said it and how quickly it was all happening. "Pet" kept floating around my head. It was a familiar word I'd encountered in high school, especially between older and younger lovers. It made sense. I was about twenty-six years old and she looked to be almost twice my age. Or maybe she was in her forties. I was not sure about how to react to the news. I did find her very attractive, but she also seemed intimidating.

In no time, we started our weekend trysts at one of her friend's hotels. She reserved a special chalet at the back of the hotel with little to no foot traffic. We had dated for more than a year when she decided to change the routine of our rendezvous. Her husband was supposed to be out of the country for a couple of weeks, so I moved into her place.

It was a weekend and she wanted us to go out for a drink since we had been holed up in the house for days on end. I had dressed up, and she was just about to put on her bra and a blouse when we heard heavy footsteps bounding up the stairs, followed by a shout of "Baby! Baby!"

I panicked and looked frantically at the open window, but she pulled me to her and asked me to crawl under the bed. In no time, her husband thumped through the door and flung it wide open. I heard the edge of the door slam into the wall.

"Baby! I have missed you so much!" he said.

"What happened? You were not supposed to be back till late next week!"

"No. I missed you so much. I couldn't wait to come back. Are you not happy to see me? Here. Some roses for you."

"You are so sweet, dear. Thank you."

I could hear the tremor in her voice. There was silence and then sounds of rough kisses. Then a thump on the bed before I heard Nelly's voice say, "Darling, you may want to take a shower before we do this."

"Does it matter? I can take a shower later."

"No, dear. Take a quick shower, and I will get a warm meal ready for when we are done. Okay?"

There was no sound, then the bed shook slightly. I didn't know what was going on. If they'd decided to have sex, I couldn't tell. I was fuming. I must have heard Nelly moan. I stifled a sneeze and wanted to pee. I squeezed my legs together to ease the pressure of the pee. But after what seemed like an eternity and they were still arguing about baths, food, and sex, and how they had missed each other, I peed on myself. It was a wooden floor, so I tried to make sure the urine was not flowing toward where they'd see it. I shifted my weight over the pool that had gathered around my crotch area and soaked up as much of the urine as I could with my trousers.

"One more kiss," I finally heard him say. His clothes dropped to the floor and then his legs darted to the bathroom.

As soon as there was a splash of water, Nelly kneeled down and whispered, "You can come out now. I am so sorry." I eased myself out from under the bed with swift moves and sauntered out of the bedroom. I didn't wait for her as she tried to throw on some clothes. Before she got downstairs, I was out of her gate and dissolved into the night. A cold wind left a chill in my spine. I felt it more on areas where my clothes were wet. I gathered my blouse closer around me and pushed ahead. Then I saw her BMW slowly circling the roundabout behind me. I dove into a corner next to the pillar of a pharmacy that was closed. I waited until she moved forward.

I didn't realize where I was until I ended up at Jibowu, a familiar area. I walked, and walked. I didn't care about the dangers of the night. I could have been killed for all I cared. There was a shift in me, and my heart was ready to bleed out and die. Knowing or being told was one thing. But being a witness was worse than I could have imagined. I knew Nelly was married, but that notion seemed so distant because I never met her husband. I was humiliated to the point of self-spite. I hated myself and loathed her even more for putting me in a position to be treated as less than an animal. Maybe we both were at fault, but I was done.

That night was the night I snapped out of the fantasy that there was ever going to be a future between us. How stupid of me to have thought of that possibility. I decided to start having sex with women I was interested in without any attachments. I was not going to be shattered the way Nelly shattered me again. I was wounded, but I had to make myself whole again from the pieces that were left of me.

The next day, I was surprised when Rosemary, the receptionist at the book club, told me that some stylish woman with a blue BMW showed up almost a dozen times looking for me. I told her that she was exaggerating. She couldn't have shown up a dozen times.

"Well, it felt like it because when it was not her asking for you, it was some man that said he was her driver. Do you owe her money?" Rosemary asked, curious.

"I don't owe her any money."

"Who is she?"

"Nobody. Mind your business."

"She gave me some money and asked me to buy myself a meal, then I was forced to promise her that I would produce you tomorrow."

"Thank you for letting me know," I told her and headed home. Anger was threatening to build up again, but I took a deep breath and told myself to be calm.

25. Threshing Floor

LUCKILY, THE DISTRACTION I needed came through a workshop sponsored by the British Council for Women Writers of Nigeria (WRITA). It was to be held at the University of Ibadan. A national tour was also part of the package. After one of the workshops at Ibadan, we had a party at one of the guest houses. It was at the party I met a bunch of interesting women. We got chatting. A couple of them stood out to me. I had never found myself in the company of so many women writers in the same space. I had to be cautious about how I approached them because my past experiences of being yelled at or slammed with the bible when I tried to be seductive always left me feeling like a thief caught in the middle of the act.

When the time came to dance, everybody paired up, man and woman. It was just me and one other girl sitting. We looked at each other and smiled. I asked her for a dance. I always found dancing with women erotic. Her rounded hips swayed back and forth. We held hands to either swirl around or to switch positions. A slow song came on, and I decided to give it a shot and tell her that she was pretty.

"So what's your name?"

"Just call me Girlie."

"Interesting name. You have a beautiful smile. I hope you don't mind when women compliment you."

"No, not at all."

"I like women a lot. What about you? You prefer men?"

"Wherever good soup drops, I lick."

My heart leaped at her response. My smile got wider, and my dance steps came with extra vigor. At the end of the dance, we found a place and smooched. That became our routine until the workshop ended.

Besides finding Girlie, I also discovered the rich library at the University of Ibadan. Under the guise of writing out folk tales, I got permission from my boss to spend weeks at Ibadan. The Ibadan library became my second home. It was there I gathered and wrote the first lesbian title essay that was published in the *Vanguard* newspaper entitled "The Emerging Lesbian Voice in Nigerian Feminist Literature." A blistering response from Kalu, who was a schoolmate from UNN and at that time was a journalist in Lagos, became the beginning of my nightmares in Lagos.

Nigeria already had a sodomy law hanging like a noose around the necks of homosexuals, but Christian and Muslim fanatics would be quick to lynch an outed homosexual. I developed heart palpitations. From verbal abuses to written notes to mailed letters, I was warned to steer clear of such a dirty lifestyle. To quell the hostility, I started dating Umar, a Hausa graduate who came from Sokoto to help his uncle with running a makeshift shop at Kilo bus stop.

Our relationship became complicated when he insisted on having sex with me. I told him I had a wound in my vagina and that if anything went in there, I would bleed. He wanted to find out for himself, and I told him that he was selfish and insensitive. Why would he want me to bleed as a way to confirm what I had told him? He agreed to keep his penis away from me and apologized, so I resorted to giving him blow jobs and playing with his penis until he reached an orgasm. Sometimes he tried thrusting his penis between my tightly closed thighs, with Vaseline. It worked for him. With time, he started asking to just dip the tip of his penis inside my vagina. We went back and forth over the same no-sex argument. Finally, we became just friends and stayed friends. There was no need to pretend that we were in a romantic relationship when he couldn't get what he wanted.

On the day I was told that I no longer had a job, I had dressed up looking forward to another day at the book club. I had taken my bath, applied my lily-scented body lotion, and sprayed a tester perfume when Christopher, my boss's house help, walked up to me and announced that my boss wanted to see me.

"What does he want me for?" I asked.

Christopher's face said nothing. The stupid boy just grinned at me. He was always giggling or grinning. Usually, I didn't mind, but that morning I found it irritating. I wanted to wipe his grin off his face.

"Do you know why he wants to see me?" I asked louder.

Christopher kept grinning. He had been nice to me, though. Late at night and also early in the mornings, he would sneak out steamy, delicious meals from our boss's kitchen for me. His kind gesture helped me save money on food, and I was grateful to him. The downside was that I often had to share my little room with stacks of plates until Christopher was finally able to fetch them.

My boss constantly needed Christopher for one thing or the other. So it was difficult to see him sometimes. When he became available, he was only always full of questions: "Unoma, why are all your friends girls? Don't you like men? Why don't you have a man to take care of you?" I would laugh it off.

On that day, I pushed Christopher aside and made for the main house. My boss was at the eating table, bare-chested. As he reached for his orange juice and napkins, his drooping belly swayed back and forth. The aroma of fried eggs and toasted bread made me drool, but I swallowed my saliva. He invited me to sit and have a meal with him.

I was too nervous to eat but also too hungry to turn down the food. I took a slice of bread, stuffed it with fried eggs and scooped it into my mouth. He ate and spoke. He had been duped out of millions and could not continue paying me. He coughed, and then he announced that he was getting ready to pack up and head to the US to be with his family. He was not exactly sure when he was going to leave, but he would give my last salary to Christopher for me. I was to check in a couple of weeks.

In silence, we continued eating as I helped myself to more slices of bread and eggs. Mr. Donatus, my boss's driver, came in with a parcel. Mr. Donatus was a tall man with a strong odor of dry sweat. His deep-etched tribal marks sank into the folds of his wide grin. He nodded when I greeted him. "Good morning, Sir," Mr. Donatus said to my boss and gave him the parcel. Without saying another word, Mr. Donatus stepped out. My boss opened the parcel, and in it were wads of dirty naira notes. Then, one Saturday afternoon, my boss suddenly closed the book club.

That was how I became homeless and jobless. I would sleep at the Association of Nigerian Authors office at Bode Thomas, battling enthusiastic mosquitoes and getting startled by every sound with the thought that the rugged gatemen had decided to break into the office and rape me. I had little sleep until my mother sent word that my older brother had found accommodation in Lagos. I moved in with him. A few weeks after I moved, Obi, a friend from the Association of Nigerian Authors, offered me a freelance job for *Vanguard* newspaper. He didn't stop at that. He found a way to get me a job interview.

On the morning I was preparing to leave for the interview, the rain poured with vigor. I stared at the falling rain, and the hysteria of the storm was rather animated. It came with quick flashes of lightning followed by deafening claps of thunder. I moved away from the window, waiting for the thunder to subside before I stepped up to the window again and exhaled as the steam assailed my face. Anthony Village was under the threat of being swallowed up by rain. Plastic bags and overturned trash were being mercilessly thrashed against walls, barricades, and fences. I was worried about my job interview at *Vanguard*. The whole street was stripped of any human life.

An hour later, the rain suddenly came to a halt. I was surprised but glad at the same time. I had one more hour to make it for the interview. I took off my shoes to wade through the flooded streets, cringing at every tingle of my feet. I could upset a floating snake or step on a nail. I had imagined a situation where electric wires were felled from their poles and electrocuted thousands of people, which could have included me. I hurried ahead as splashes of dirty brown water soaked the edges of my black skirt.

It was a relief to find a waiting bus as soon as I got to the Anthony bus stop. The lean conductor gave me his seat and called out for more passengers. The guy sitting next to me smiled and handed me a pamphlet before letting me know that Jesus loves me. I thanked him and took the pamphlet. He cleared his throat and started screeching about how the fire and brimstone that would destroy the world this time was going to be worse than Sodom and Gomorrah because the sins of this generation had superseded those of the biblical cities.

It was not just the volume of his ear-splitting sermon that bothered me. Every bit of his spittle seemed to be concentrating on my neck. I couldn't bear it. It was either I ask the bus driver to stop or find a way to change seats, so I pleaded with the conductor to take my seat while I sat opposite him on top of where their spare batteries were kept. Instantly, I felt the near burning warmth of the seat and wriggled in discomfort until I got to Ojota where I took a bus to Mile 2.

In my attempt to avoid the dirty water buses splashed as they sped past, I almost fell into an overflowing gutter. I did avoid falling, but I was not too lucky as a huge blotch of water landed on my pelvic area. I could smell the stale odor of urine mixed with shit. I cursed the bus and for a minute contemplated going back home to change clothes, but I kept on. A throng of people stood around waiting for buses. Some tried to negotiate their ways around pools and gushing water from overflowing gutters. Most of them held onto their shoes while others gathered the edges of their cloth in their hands as they made their way to dry areas.

Inside the Mile 2 bus, I had a heart palpitation. It had gotten worse after the homosexual article I wrote in *Vanguard*. The threats to my life got close to home because even some fellow members of the ANA seemed angry about my strange and disgusting ideas about homosexuality. My job loss also made the heart palpitation uncontrollable. Staying in touch and updating Leslye Huff, the woman I saw as the river goddess, Onishe, in human flesh, helped because she often called me at my friend's house. Oma would usually be the one to let me know whenever she called. Because of the time difference, I sometimes slept on their couch beside the phone.

I also constantly sent her email. My friend Kole, who was a photographer, helped me by letting me use his external modem and a phone to retrieve documents and emails from Leslye. He saved the messages on a floppy disk and then printed them out for me at a business center for a fairly affordable fee. Leslye often sent me money, so that helped. She assisted by also giving my work a platform in the United States, so much so that some of my works got the attention of a human rights organization in New York, and that earned me an award.

26. Birds Above the Canal

T HE CONDUCTOR'S SHOUT of "Mile 2 don dey reach o!" yanked me out of my reverie when the bus slammed into a deep pothole and dirty water splashed up onto my forehead. It trickled down my nose, and I could smell the stench of musty fruits and feces. I wiped my face with both of my palms before it trickled down into my mouth.

At Mile 2, the traffic was less hectic. Overgrown grasses straddled both sides of the road and there were fewer pedestrians. Through the window, I could see a solitary teenage girl with a tray of oranges on her head. "Buy oranges! Sweet oranges!" she wailed.

"Canal! Canal!" the bus conductor called out.

Canal was my bus stop. I tapped him on his shoulder to let him know that I was stopping at Canal, which led to the path for *Vanguard*. I wanted to see Obi first to see if he'd approve an event I wanted to cover at Opebi-Allen. The receptionist told me that he was at their restaurant. There, he fed me and wished me luck with the interview.

In the office where the interview was to be held, the windows were closed, and the air conditioning hummed in the background. Mr. Ode, the interviewer, greeted me, and the interview started with basic questions about my qualifications, experience, and passion for journalism. Then he informed me that he wanted to send me on a couple of assignments first and we would take it from there.

I was about to step out of his office when he asked me if I had a boyfriend, and I lied that I did. Such questions only led to one thing: sex. He looked me in the eye and told me that he could take care of me better than my boyfriend did, that I should not be in a hurry to give him a response. I should take my time to think about it. There and then, I knew that I was not going to get or find a permanent job with him. I tried to find Obi on my way out, but didn't. I left the building.

Outside, the rain had lessened to a drizzle. I flagged down an *okada*. The motorbike's wheels left a trail of mud on my left leg as we zoomed off.

I got to Opebi-Allen Avenue where I was to cover an event organized by a women's rights group; it seemed to be one of the busiest streets in Lagos. There were rumors that it was one of the most vibrant red-light districts in Lagos. Some high-end companies and offices were located there. Elite homes were also located there. When I got inside the venue, the event looked more like a birthday bash. I approached one of the ladies I saw, who told me it was a convention party for the Women Against Violence Society; she escorted me in. The secretary was in her office taking an important call from the vice president of the organization. She invited me to sit in the large living room and said she would call the vice president to meet me while I waited.

A lot of women were milling around. Most of them were quite attractive, and I tried not to stare too hard. I flipped through the bundle of magazines laid out on a side table. I was excited about my first major assignment: getting a personal interview with the president of one of the women's rights organizations or any of the high-ranking women in the organization. When the lady came back with the secretary of the organization, I was told to sign their guest book and show some kind of ID. I did. Then I ended up in the president's office, which was near empty. Except for the chair beside a huge table in the middle of the room, there was only one other chair and a side table with a lamp on it.

"Make yourself comfortable!" She was a tall and elegant woman who might have been in her early fifties. Her makeup looked natural and well blended into her skin. She was a gorgeous woman with a warm smile.

"They said there is a journalist here waiting to interview me. That must be you?"

"Yes," I said.

"What's your name?"

"Unoma."

"Nice name!"

For some reason, a lot of images ran through my mind from the relentless rain to the smell of shit on my clothes. As much as I tried to dismiss the odor, it kept tormenting me. Or, maybe I had become self-conscious in Madam President's presence.

I had turned on my recorder on her table and was ready with the first question when the rain started again. It sounded as if pebbles were dropping on the roof of the building. The room became darker, but she didn't want us to use the office next to hers. She got up and parted the lush curtains on her window. There was more light, and she sat down. There were a couple of framed pictures on her table. She noticed I was looking at a photo and told me that it was her with her best friend in the university. There was something intimate about the way they posed in the picture. They were probably more than friends. Why was it not her husband's picture on the table? There were no pictures of a family with her, her kids, and her husband. She had the same picture with her best friend in three different locations in the office. They were not conspicuous, but if anyone cared to look hard enough, they were noticeable. I looked at the frame closer to me and smiled. She asked me if I recognized her best friend, and I said no, but that her best friend reminded me of my lover.

We were halfway through the interview when the rain worsened and the room got dark again. She asked if I minded going to a more comfortable place, and I didn't mind. With a large umbrella, she led me to her car and around to the passenger's side. Then she went around to the driver's side and half got in. She was about to fold up her umbrella, which she held above her, when the gateman ran out into the rain and held it for her. She thanked him and then fumbled for her purse inside a large handbag wedged between the gear levers and my seat. She gave him a one-thousand-naira note. The echo of "Thank you, ma! Thank you, ma!" rang through the rain.

Just a few houses down the same street, we pulled into a modest house with well-trimmed hedges. The president said it was her guesthouse. Inside was a lavish, well-furnished living room. I hesitated before stepping onto the rug and pulled off my shoes. She dropped her handbag on the longest couch in the room and excused herself. Right opposite me was a minibar. I sat back and inhaled the most pleasant rose fragrance I'd ever experienced. Within minutes, Madam President was out. She had on a yellow, free-flowing gown.

"Are you hungry?" she asked.

"Not really. I wouldn't mind a drink, though."

"Wine, malt, soft drink?"

"Wine or gin would be perfect."

"For wine, white, red?"

"Red."

She invited me to her bar and told me about all the types of wine, their history, and why older wines taste the best. I was impressed by her knowledge. She poured some wine for me, and we settled into the interview. She told me to take my time. She would drop me off if it got too late, or I could sleep over. For some reason, I couldn't look straight into her eyes. The radiance of her beautiful face seemed too bright to behold. Maybe it was the wine, but I hadn't drunk that much. I tried to pull myself together.

Her name was Gloria, which she insisted I call her. She was married but separated temporarily from her husband. She lived her life as a single mother. She had schooled and lived in the US for years before deciding to come home and give back. Gloria asked me about myself: where I was from, what I had studied at the university, how long I had been a journalist, my plans, and if I enjoyed my job. My eyes darted around. They went everywhere except her face. At a point, I started slurring my words. She asked if I was all right. I didn't respond, so she kneeled before me and held my face. I don't know where I found the courage, but I gave her a lingering kiss. I think the light in the room dimmed at that moment.

When I left the next morning, I was wasted. Gloria desperately wanted to take me home, but I refused. I was too embarrassed to spend another minute in her presence. But I loved the glow in my groin. I wobbled my way to Opebi-Allen junction to find a bus back to Anthony Village. That was it. I just wanted a fling. Another Nelly was not going to happen to me.

With freelance jobs, I was able to sustain myself and throw my whole weight into my job as the assistant secretary for ANA. For days, when I needed to do my ANA duties, Mr. Bajo was always supportive with money and meals. The whole ANA clan that included Anke of the Goethe Institute, Ogaga, Odia, Lola, Akachi, Angela, Maik, Otiono, Toni, Nike, Funmi, Lookman, Raji, Pius, Chiedu, Sanya, Lasisi, Jahman, Promise, Maik, Lynn, Akin, Kole, EC, Mike, Maxim, Akachi, Mobolaji, Toyin, Omowunmi, and many others, seemed to always huddle together for a variety of literary and art events in Lagos and Ibadan.

Amongst us, there was strong passion for art, creativity, poetry, fiction, journalism, and thirst for life and romance. We mostly got along except for when any of them expressed a romantic interest to me. Lynn became my closest ally and protector. It was to her I ran to about threats to my life and vengeful grudges from the men I had turned down. My life as a lesbian out to a community of writers and struggling to navigate my way through the muddy waters of hate and homophobia, she had said, inspired her to write a novel, *The Man*, about a homosexual man whom she saw in my shoes. And so our conversation about my life, our lives, and her attempt to capture homosexual narratives among writers, scholars, and friends initiated a great friendship and inspiring dialogues amongst us. Though she stood the risk of being labeled a lesbian because of our friendship, she stood by my side.

I had friends like Ola who didn't want to be directly involved with LGBT rights because, as she said, it was not her fight and that until gay people decided to organize and become activists, nobody else was going to do it for them. I was disappointed and felt betrayed. I suppose that because she looked androgynous, people did spread rumors that we were lovers. She seemed entertained by the buzz, yet I felt for some reason, she was sitting on the fence when it came to LGBT rights. Her attitude reminded me of a line from Dylan's "The Times They Are A' Changing", which Lynn shared with me.

I remained resolute to keep pushing forward and to keep proclaiming my existence. I was elated when Promise offered me the opportunity to research for her literary journal. I had the chance to return to Ibadan again, back to the Women's Development Center, which had one of the richest collections of gender and feminist textbooks. I practically slept in that library, which was said to have been founded by Bolanle Awe, an accomplished scholar.

I was so absorbed in reading and discovering books that I realized I needed to spend more time at Ibadan. So when Funmi, one of the friends I made during the Women Writers workshop at Ibadan, made the offer for me to stay in her one-bedroom student apartment, it was a dream come true. We shared her mattress, a stove and some pots, pans, and plates for meager but sustaining meals.

It was at the Women's Development Center that I read and explored intriguing and fresh voices like Temi, Lola, and Promise, who were breaking through a new terrain in Nigerian literature through their intrepid venture into gay writing. It was their narratives that motivated me to start researching and building an LGBT body of work.

Part of what made the Association of Nigerian Authors' family lively with all its drama and drive were special moments that included writing competitions, gossips, in-fighting, and love affairs. Some of these dramas included press attacks about older writers calling some young poets professional bachelors. I found myself often in Lynn's company sharing glasses of beer and talking deep into the night about how Nigeria dealt with difference and its lack of affirming difference. And how we dealt with disability and the worst disability being the hidden kind and the psychological damage we caused others by rejecting them.

I maintained a low-key presence and carried on with freelancing and testing new waters in queer writing, but I experienced the first physical homophobic attack when I was ambushed at Anthony bus stop by two men in a semi-dark corner under the bridge. I made a frantic call to Leslye Huff. She was able to secure a scholarship for a Master's program in English in Ohio for me. While I applied for a visa and waited for it to be processed, I kept a low profile and got back home while it was still daylight. My attendance at events got less and less, and everybody became a suspect. My level of paranoia increased so that even close friends noticed and would advise me to talk less about issues surrounding homosexuality. I had lived for so long with mental and psychological abuse that I began to believe that I deserved all the pain I endured. I had no rights.

On the day my plane lifted from Lagos, I looked down and felt the throb of all my wounds. For a city that was constantly plunged into darkness because of power failure, there was so much blazing light. An elusive light I needed to leave to be able to look at it in perspective. I took a last glance at a city and a country I had known all my life. With deep and shallow scars, I looked forward and soared. My thoughts steadied. There was a turbulence.

***

But America had waiting surprises. There is homophobia. They also fling bibles at queer bodies for cleansing. There is racism. *There is... There is...* New battles teach me new survival skills. I become the "other" in the "other" while navigating the razor-sharp margins of this new home.

Author's Note

Some names and location have been changed to protect some of the people in my memoir who are still alive and may be exposed to attacks and scandals because of my revelations.

Anu Lakhan and Debbie McGowan, thank you for your time and for believing.

About the Author

Unoma Azuah teaches writing at Wiregrass Georgia Technical College, Valdosta, GA. Her research and activism focus on Lesbian, Gay, Bisexual, and Transgender (LGBT) rights in Nigeria, and her most recent book project is *Blessed Body: Secret Lives of the Nigerian LGBT*. Some of her writing awards include the Aidoo-Synder book award, Spectrum book award, and the Hellman/Hammet award.

Social Media:

Website: https://unomaazuah.net
Facebook: https://www.facebook.com/unoma.azuah
Twitter: @unomaazuah

By the Author

Critical Essays:

"Poetry, Religion, and Empowerment in Nigerian Lesbian Self-Writing," *The African Journal of Gender and Religion*, vol. 25, no. 1, 2019.

"Nigeria." *The Global Encyclopedia of Lesbian, Gay, Bisexual, and Transgender History will provide a global view of the history of LGBTQ*, Edited by Howard Chiang, Anjali Arondekar, Marc Epprecht, et al. Charles Scribner's Sons: Gale, A Cengage Company, 2019.

"Visual Activism for the African LGBT: a look at the documentary 'Born This Way,'" *A Journal of African Literature Today*: 36, Queer Theory in African Fiction and Film, 2018.

"Celebrating Area Scatter, the drag Queen that Transgressed Gender Roles in South-East Nigeria," in *Reclaiming Afrikan: Queer Perspectives on Sexual and Gender Identities*, edited by Zethu Matebeni, Modjaji Books, 2014.

"The Video Closet: Nollywood's Gay-Themed Movies," *Transition*, vol. 106, no. 1, 2012.

"Extortion and Blackmail of Nigerian Lesbians and Bisexual Women," in *Nowhere to Turn: Blackmail and Extortion of LGBT People in Sub-Saharan Africa*, edited by Ryan Thoreson & Sam Cook, International Gay and Lesbian Human Rights Commission, 2011.

"Nigeria," *The Greenwood Encyclopedia of LGBT Issues Worldwide*, vol. 1, edited by Chuck Stewart, ABC-CLIO press, 2010.

"Same-Sex Sexuality Issues in Some African Popular Media," *Canadian Journal of African Studies*, vol. 43. no. 1, 2009.

"Women Writers' Round Table: Of Phases and Faces: Unoma Azuah engages Sefi Attah and Chika Unigwe," *Research in African Literatures*, vol. 39, no. 2, 2008. [interview]

"Emerging Lesbian Voice in the Nigerian feminist Literature," *Body, Gender and Sexuality*, edited by Flora Veit-Wild & Dirk Naguschewski, Matatu Press, 2005.

Novels:

Embracing My Shadow: growing up lesbian in Nigeria, Beaten Track Publishing, 2020. [non-fiction]

Sky-high Flames, Cookingpot Publishing, 2018.

Edible Bones, Demarche Publishing, 2013.

Anthologies:

Mounting the Moon: Queer Nigerian Poems, Cookingpot Publishing, 2018.

On Broken Wings: An Anthology of Best Contemporary Nigerian Poetry, Cookingpot Publishing, 2018.

Blessed Body: The Secret Lives of LGBT Nigerians, Cookingpot Publishing, 2017.

The Length of Light, a Collection of Short Stories, VDM Verlag Dr. Müller, 2008.

Night Songs, a Collection of Poetry, Oracle Books, 2002.

Stories and Poems:

"Where Men Dwell," in *Routledge Handbook of Queer African Studies*, edited by S.N. Nyeck, Routledge Publishers, 2020. [poem]

"Staying Afloat," in *Queer Africa 2: New Stories*, edited by Makhosazana Xaba and Karen Martin, MaThoko Books, 2018.

Audio version:
https://www.iheart.com/podcast/256-nipe-story-31035528/
episode/staying-afloat-by-unoma-azuah-46341880/

"Dots of Lineage Lines," *Panorama: the Journal of Intelligent Travel*, 2016. [poem]

"Molding Memories," in *Anthology of New Works by African Women Poets*, edited by Antonia Kalu et al., Lynn Rienner, 2013. [poem]

"The Shedding of Blood," in *African Sexualities: A Reader*, edited by S. Tamale, 2011, Fahamu and Pambazuka Press, 2011. [poem]

"Stations of the Core," in *Sentinel Literature Festival Anthology*, edited by Unoma Azuah, Amanda Sington-Williams, and Nnorom Azuonye , SPM press, 2010. [poem]

"Lady Chatterley's Mansion," *The New Black Magazine*, 2010. [short story]

"Learning to walk on black Ice," *Farafina Literary Magazine*, 2008. [non-fiction]

"Seasons of Scorch," *Beate Sigriddaughter* (online literary magazine), winter 2007. [short story]

"Walking into my Groom," in *Weaverbird Collection: New Fiction from Nigeria*, edited by Sarah Ladipo Manyika, Farafina Publishers, 2007. [short story]

"Arrivals" Stylusrespond.com (online literary magazine), November 2006. [poem]

"Tropical Rain" and "Aevum," *Karogs Journal*, 2006. [poems]

"Green Slime," *Karavan*, 2006. [poem]

"Onishe," "Leaving Lagos," "Alien," "Home Is Where the Heart Hurts," and "On the throne of Grace," *The Other Voices International Project*, 2005. [poems]

"Erico," *16 Nigerian Women Writers, an anthology of short stories,* edited by Toyin Adewale-Gabriel, Ishmael Reed Publications, 2005. [short story]

"Bulging Bag," *GUMBO, an anthology of African American writing*, edited by Golden, Harrison, Harlem Moon, 2002. [short story]

"Forbidden," *25 New Nigerian Poets*, edited by Toyin Adewale-Nduka, Ishmael Reed Publications, 2000. [poem]

Beaten Track Publishing

For more titles from Beaten Track Publishing,
please visit our website:

https://www.beatentrackpublishing.com

Thanks for reading!

CPSIA information can be obtained
at www.ICGtesting.com
Printed in the USA
LVHW040616230122
709144LV00007B/705

9 781786 453730